Cooking Adventures with Michael Field

Pies, Tarts, and Chou Puffs

American Pies—An International Heritage

Tarts and Tartlets—A Franco-American Alliance

Cream Puffs and Savory Puffs

Nelson Doubleday, Inc.   Garden City, New York

Introduction

The common denominator linking such enticing culinary terms as pies, tarts, and *chou* puffs is the word *paste*. And paste—whether it is called pastry in English, *pâte* in French, *pasticceria* in Italian, or *pastelería* in Spanish—is a comparatively flavorless composition of flour, fat, and liquid, and, on occasion, eggs. This simple mixture has been prepared and baked in one form or another for centuries—the German *strudel,* the paper-thin Greek *phylo,* or the many-leaved French puff pastry, *feuilletage,* are only a few examples —and has been used as a base for many of the world's most glamorous, elaborate, and sustaining dishes.

Although the international guises that pastry can take are virtually limitless, I am concerned in this book with my versions of four classic pas-

tries that are as satisfying and delicious as any you can imagine.

You will find in this book basic pastries used for flaky-crusted American pies, for French tarts and tartlets with velvety fillings, and for puffs as fragile and as ephemeral as the air they contain. You will discover, too, the appropriate fillings for pastry constructions to be served as *hors-d'oeuvre,* main dishes, and desserts.

The homely saying "easy as pie" may be oversimplifying matters a bit, but when you really know what you are doing in pastry making the simile will be apt. The techniques of making simple doughs, wielding a rolling pin, and baking pastries are by no means as complicated as cooks —novice and skilled—too often feel them to be. In spite of how much your mother or your grandmother may have intimidated you by the phrase "a light hand with pastry," your successes, like theirs, will depend more on precision and practice than on any God-given gift for pastry making.

When, after you have read the following pages, you embark on making what may perhaps be your first pie, tart, or puff, you will find yourself sailing on fully charted seas; I have left little to chance.

Your laden ship of pastry may on occasion tend to leak a bit at the seams, it may graze an unexpected shoal or two, and it may even threaten to founder altogether, but don't give up the ship. If you keep your eye on my culinary compass— or, less metaphorically, follow my recipes to the letter—your disasters (if any) will be few. Even a less-than-perfect outcome of any recipe in the book will be superior to most of the gummy pies and tarts and cardboard-textured puffs that you may have been buying in your supermarket or bakery. I think it is time for us all to bring baking back into the home kitchen where it really belongs, and where we can make delectable pastries easily, honestly, and joyfully.

Know Your Oven

The first word that comes to my mind when baking is mentioned is *oven*. Most of us take ovens—commonplace equipment in even the simplest kitchens—very much for granted, but the behavior of ovens, whether fueled by gas or electricity, can vary surprisingly. Fortunately, however old or errant your oven, there is a simple way to make it perform as it should.

Temperature Control

Primarily, you need to be concerned with the proper functioning of your oven thermostat, or oven control. It *must* control the heat as it says it is doing—in other words, it must be accurate to within a few degrees. There is nothing more catastrophic than assuming that you are baking a pie at 375° and then discovering too late, to your horror, that the pastry has burned to a crisp because, unbeknownst to you, it has been baking at a much higher temperature, perhaps even at 475°. Such a thermostat problem is easily remedied by having your oven calibrated. Ask your local utility company or a range serviceman to check your oven control, and have it adjusted whenever it seems necessary.

As a further guarantee of oven performance, it is worth the small investment to buy an oven thermometer (Taylor and Tel-Tru are among the good brands). Keep it suspended from one of the racks in the center of the oven, not near the side or front. At a glance, then, you will be able to tell whether your oven control is functioning as it should.

How to Handle Hot Spots

Despite the care lavished upon the construction and insulation of ovens for the even distribution of heat, there is still a possibility that some areas of your oven may be hotter than others. Resign yourself to the fact that nothing can be done about this unfortunate "hot-spot" phenomenon—that is, mechanically at least.

Recognition of any hot spots will come when you find that your pastry is not browning evenly. The best way to cope with this is simply to shift whatever pie, tart, or tartlet you are baking to a place in your oven where the heat is more evenly distributed. Or, you might take advantage of a hot spot and turn your pie or tart around from time to time until all sides are evenly browned. Unfortunately, *chou* puffs are more fragile than pies and tarts and are not so easily managed. They must rise completely before being moved.

The Ingredients for Pies, Tarts, and *Chou* Puffs—Preferences and Prejudices

My preferences and prejudices are not as capricious or willful as you might, at first glance, suppose. They do, it is true, represent my personal response to the taste of food. More important, however, is the fact that they reflect my preoccupation with predictable cooking; my recommendations are for the most part based upon that alone.

Preferences...

FLOUR

The recipes in this book require all-purpose flour—not cake flour, or self-rising flour, or bread flour, or instant (granulated) flour, or pastry flour.

All-purpose flours are available throughout the United States and are sold under many brand names. They all look alike (except for a difference in the degree of whiteness between bleached and unbleached all-purpose flours), but they have subtly different characteristics that are neither described on their labels nor apparent to the eye. The differences—which include varying proportions of hard and soft wheat, the presence or absence of enrichment, the various processes by which each brand is milled—are usually of importance only to the nutritionist or professional pastry maker.

To assure you of as much predictability as possible in the recipes in this book, I have used the same brand (Gold Medal) consistently, not because of any intrinsic superiority of that flour to other all-purpose flours, but simply because it is readily available. And I would suggest that you either use Gold Medal, or that you experiment with other brands until you find one that gives you consistently good results.

There is, however, one factor in all-purpose flour which may be of importance to you which I would like to touch upon briefly.

Gluten

Loosely defined, gluten is a substance composed of protein elements present in varying amounts in all wheat flours. And whatever the amount of gluten in your brand of all-purpose flour, it will develop a certain amount of elasticity in every pastry you make. To return to the time-worn cliché "a light hand with pastry," it means more precisely speed and dexterity in mixing, handling, and rolling pastry to prevent it from developing too much elasticity—the common cause of tough crusts.

FATS

For every one of my pie, tart, tartlet, or *chou*-paste recipes you will be using solid vegetable shortening or butter, either separately or in combination, for a simple reason: vegetable shortening and butter produce the best pastries—flaky, rich, and easy to handle before baking.

Butter

Except in American pie crusts, I am unconditionally committed to butter for most cooking purposes— but particularly for tarts and puffs. And I am even more committed to sweet butter (that is, butter made from sweet cream, but free of salt). However, salt butter (that is, butter made from sweet cream to which salt is added) is also acceptable, and if you prefer it, as so many Americans do, reduce the salt called for in my recipes for tart and *chou* pastries by half.

There are some curious yet relevant facts I think you should know about butter in general. The U.S. Department of Agriculture grades or "scores" butter on the basis of

such factors as aroma, texture, and flavor.

The best butter, made of sweet cream, is scored AA, the next best, A —and the package is so marked. You may also find butter scored by number, and the number 93 (for reasons unfathomable to me) is the equivalent of AA, and 92 is the equivalent of A. However, the Department of Agriculture is now discouraging the use of numbers, and numbered scoring is slowly but surely being replaced by the more logical letters. Should you find butter scored B— and occasionally you may in some small towns—it will (or at least it should) be labeled as being made from sour, or so-called "ripened," cream. Despite its slightly acidulated flavor this somewhat inferior butter may be used in any of my recipes that require butter.

Never use the product called whipped butter for pastry making. Although it serves well enough as a spread, the air whipped into it re-

places a part of the fat, reducing its shortening power and changing its texture so that it will make only a leaden and rather oily pastry.

Vegetable Shortening

Made from bland vegetable oils, vegetable shortening is generally white or creamy in color. It has little or no flavor; it needn't be refrigerated; and it keeps almost indefinitely without deteriorating.

The standard brands—Crisco, for example—contain no animal fats, and most vegetable shortenings are now being produced by methods that keep their content of saturated fats as low as possible. Polysaturated fats are considered nutritionally undesirable nowadays, for reasons having to do with cholesterol levels in the blood—a matter still being investigated by scientists, with far from conclusive results.

EGGS

Eggs are used in my tartlet pastry,

in my custard fillings for pies and tarts, in my lemon meringue pie, and as a puffing agent in *chou* paste. It is important for you to note that when I specify eggs in my recipes, I always mean U.S. Standard "large" eggs, which weigh 24 ounces to the dozen. Should you substitute small, medium, extra-large, or jumbo eggs, you may find the mathematical adjustments involved almost as insurmountable as they are to me. Any miscalculation will upset the balance I have created to insure your recipes turning out as they should.

The freshness of eggs is important to the success of many dishes, but in making pastries and fillings it is not essential that the eggs be new-laid. In fact, eggs a few days old are preferable to really fresh eggs when you hard-cook them, or when you use egg whites for meringues. And as for the whole eggs you will use in custard fillings, their age will make very little difference, if any at all, in the final result.

SUGAR

When sugar is indicated in any recipe in this book, as it is in sweet fillings for pies, tarts, and puffs, it will be for the most part the standard type of granulated sugar.

There will, however, be instances where other sugars are specified, and you should never substitute one for another. When I say light-brown or dark-brown sugar I do not mean "Brownulated" sugar, or granulated brown sugar, which pours easily, but behaves rather unpredictably in

cooking, to say the least.

In my recipes, confectioners' sugar (which contains about 3 per cent cornstarch, added to prevent caking) is primarily used as a powdery and decorative dusting agent. You may be confused when shopping for it because it is sometimes referred to in the vernacular as "powdered sugar," but it is labeled on packages as XXXX or 10X confectioners' sugar. Consolingly, whatever the designation, they are one and the same—confectioners' sugar.

THICKENINGS

Most pie fillings, especially those made with fruit, need a thickening agent to help prevent the bottom crust from becoming soggy and to make it possible to cut the finished pie into fairly compact but still juicy sections.

The best thickeners for fruit-filled pies are cornstarch, arrowroot, tapioca, and flour. In each recipe I recommend a specific thickener for a specific fruit. Cornstarch, arrowroot, and tapioca can be used interchangeably in the same amounts to achieve more or less the same density of the finished filling. If you use flour in place of one of these, it is necessary to use twice the amount to achieve the same result.

LIQUIDS

All pastry requires moisture of some sort to make the particles of flour adhere to each other. And water (iced, to prevent the fat in the pastry from softening too much) is the most reliable binding element. Some cooks mistakenly believe that a substitute for water—fruit juice, for example—will improve the flavor of the pastry. Not only will the fruit flavor be virtually lost in the pastry, but the acidity of the juice, if it is used in a sufficient quantity to replace water, may break down the structure of the flour and make the pastry, whatever its type, almost impossible to handle.

...and Some Prejudices

LARD

Some of you may like the flavor of lard—and it is indeed a distinctive one when used in pastry. Unfortunately, most packaged lard today has been so emulsified, hydrogenated, and refined to insure its stability that few brands, if any, have the special flavor and richness of old-fashioned leaf lard, almost impossible to find now.

However, if you insist upon using ordinary packaged lard, it may be substituted for vegetable shortening in precisely the same amounts. Or you can combine shortening and lard in any proportion you like. I would suggest, however, that you do not experiment with substitutions until you have mastered my pastry-making techniques, using the ingredients specified in the recipes.

OILS

Erase from your mind any recipes you may have read which suggest us-ing vegetable oils in place of solid fat. Pastries made with oil—for my palate, at least—leave a great deal to be desired, and the results do not justify learning the techniques involved.

MARGARINE

You may substitute margarine for butter, if for any reason you *must* use it. It will produce inferior but still palatable pastry. Margarine is made by emulsifying oil (usually vegetable oil, although some margarines contain animal fats) with cultured milk, then kneading the resulting fat to a consistency similar to that of butter. Margarine has no flavor except what it gains from being churned with the milk, plus artificial flavorings.

I shun margarine entirely. From my point of view, there is nothing more delicious than the flavor of pure butter.

PASTRY MIXES

Instant pie-crust mixes are dubious preparations that bear only a slight resemblance to the real thing. Furthermore, my American pie crust prepared from scratch is cheaper, better, and not much more difficult to make. And as for my tart and tartlet pastries, I seriously doubt if anything even remotely approaching them is available in a mix. Unfortunately, however, there are cream-puff mixes on the market that have the same defects as pie-crust mixes. Needless to say, I would avoid them.

PACKAGED AND CANNED FILLINGS

I have no enthusiasm for packaged or fully cooked, canned pie fillings —admittedly convenient to use. To my mind they are generally tasteless and overly thickened and have synthetic overtones. In the absence of fresh fruit, frozen fruit, thoroughly defrosted and drained, makes an excellent substitute. As for canned fruits, sour red cherries canned in water are the only kind I really prefer for pies.

The Crucial Importance of Sifting and Measuring Your Flour

Always sift flour before measuring it unless otherwise directed. Then spoon the sifted flour lightly into a dry-measuring cup and scrape off the surplus with the back of a knife.

Most all-purpose flour is labeled "presifted"; this would appear to make flour sifting superfluous. But dry ingredients, especially flour, tend to settle (which means that they increase in density) when kept very

long or when stored in a damp atmosphere. So play it safe and always sift flour (except that used for dusting) before measuring it.

Remember, too, that when you combine two or more dry ingredients, sifting them together will insure mixing them completely. You couldn't possibly achieve such uniformity were you to merely stir the ingredients together with a spoon or a whisk.

But I must repeat my caution that you should never rap the cup containing the flour in order to make it meet the level required for your recipe. To do so will increase the quantity of flour disastrously.

The Temperature of Pastry Ingredients

To be sure that any ingredients that should be chilled will be at the correct temperature, *read the recipe completely before you begin.* Following this bit of simple-sounding advice will help to insure the success of your flaky pastry.

American pies for all seasons. Top, a deep-dish pie of frozen blueberries. Center, a latticed pie of canned cherries. Bottom, apple pie made with fresh fruit.

American Pies — An International Heritage

Had the serpent in the Garden of Eden tempted Eve with a golden-crusted apple pie instead of an apple, he might have hastened Adam's fall. The consequences notwithstanding, temptation lingers on. How else to account for the persistent passion so many of us have for apples—especially when they have been baked in a pie?

Almost every country in the world has for centuries taken pride in its pies—whatever they were filled with, or no matter how bizarre or multitudinous their shapes.

There is the Moroccan *bastila*, consisting of tissue-thin layers of pastry, sometimes triangular, filled with pigeon meat and aromatic spices; the French *pâté en croûte,* a rectangular box of pastry filled with a compact mixture of ground meats with herb seasonings; the Italian *pizza* (often called "pizza pie"—an amusing redundancy, since *pizza,* literally, means pie), made of a bread dough stretched thin and masked with a piquant tomato and cheese topping and often adorned with sausage, anchovies, olives, mushrooms, or anything else the Italian housewife may have on hand.

But the English, whose cuisine is perhaps the most maligned of any in the world, have surely, with their beef and kidney pies, their mincemeat pies inseparable from Christmas, their deep apple pies baked in a bowl, their pillow-shaped Cornish pasties, and such conceits as latticed parsnip pies festooned with primroses, raised pie making to its most fanciful and poetic heights. That is, until the Americans came along.

The Emergence of the True American Pie

Almost from the beginning, America, with an inexhaustible bounty of fruit and vegetables at hand, produced pies that were increasingly different from those of other countries. Little by little American cooks modified, simplified, and transformed the pastry-making principles brought from their ancestral homelands until, by some mysterious alchemy, the typical shallow, circular, flaky-crusted American pie, as we know it today, evolved.

Despite the endless array in cookbooks today—even good cookbooks—of recipes for pie pastry made with hot water, oil, eggs, cream cheese, and whatnot, I am convinced that early American cooks knew what they were doing when they kept their pastry as simple as possible and used only flour, shortening, salt, and water. I have therefore concentrated on what I consider to be a fine, successful, standard American pastry recipe; and you will find various adaptations of it for double-crusted pies, deep-dish pie lids, and fully baked shells. This pastry is without a doubt one of the easiest to handle, and you will find it invaluable once you have mastered it.

Although we think of most standard American pies as two-crusted—that is, consisting of a lower and an upper crust, sealed together to enclose a filling and baked in a pan—this does little justice to Yankee (or for that matter, Southern) ingenuity. Apple pies were not alone in the flowering of the pie maker's art. American cooks experimented with (and often perfected) fruit pies of every description, to say nothing of chiffon pies, custard pies, pecan pies, lemon pies, and other pies without end—all as American as the land which produced them.

The pies in this book are in the same tradition—simplified, expanded, or even enriched to reflect the new bounty provided by new equipment, better refrigeration, freezing methods, and, I must admit however immodestly, often my own ingenuity.

Utensils You Will Need for Pies . . .

Pastry Blender   This ingenious instrument is especially useful in making my pastry for American pies. Try to find one with a handle that is welded to the wire blade rather than one secured with a small nut and bolt, which more often than not will fly apart under the stress of use. If you have a nut-and-bolt model, tighten the nut from time to time.

Pastry Cloth and Rolling-Pin Sleeve
The most common cause of despair
in pastry making is having your pastry stick to the rolling surface. To
prevent this from happening, I recommend a heavy canvas pastry cloth
and an open-ended stockinette rolling-pin sleeve. Both are washable
and are usually sold as a set. The
cloths come in a variety of sizes, but
the most practical for making pies
(and tarts, too) is about 20 × 24
inches. *If you are gadget-minded,
the Foley Manufacturing Company
makes a cloth that has circles outlined in red on its surface and pock-
ets that hold rods at either end. The
marks guide you when you roll out
the pastry and the rods hold the
cloth flat during use.*

Rolling Pin   Buy a heavy one with
a pin about 10 inches long and 2
inches in diameter, either an old-
fashioned but excellent one-piece
design or a ball-bearing pin that re-
volves between its handles.

Pie Pans   I firmly recommend dull-
finished aluminum pie pans. These,
unlike pans with gleaming surfaces,
absorb heat evenly and therefore
produce deeper browning. Buy at
least two. I prefer those made by
Wear-Ever which are 9 inches in diameter at the top (inside measurement) and 1¼ inches deep. Their
extended rims, about ½ inch wide,
make for more securely constructed
pies.

A 9-inch ovenproof glass pie plate
is also recommended, specifically for
my deep-dish fruit pies, although it
can be used for the chilled crumb
crust as well.

For those of you who prefer individual deep-dish fruit pies, choose
8 small (5- or 6-ounce) or 4 large (10-
ounce) heatproof dishes made of
either glass or pottery.
*Because glass retains heat so persist-
ently I do not recommend glass pie
plates for standard single-crusted or
double-crusted pies. The bottom
crust seldom browns as evenly as I*

like, and the filling frequently over-cooks. Moreover, glass pie plates are generally deeper than the 9-inch aluminum pans for which my recipes have been devised.

1½-Quart Soufflé Dish   You will need a dish precisely 3 inches deep and 7½ inches in diameter (inside measurement). There are many uses for this dish (one of them, obviously, for soufflés). It is, however, indispensable for making the Deep-Dish Chicken Pie in this book.

Mixing Bowls   A set of three is recommended (small, medium, and large), preferably of stainless steel, but definitely not aluminum.

Double Boiler   The inset (or top pan) should be of 3-quart capacity. Stainless steel is ideal, but it can be expensive and is sometimes difficult to find. Considerably less expensive enameled pans, while they may chip and tend to be lightweight, are, in general, quite satisfactory. Glass double boilers should be avoided: they are not only breakable, but retain heat so persistently that they make cooking control difficult.

Heavy 12-Inch Frying Pan with a Nonstick Surface and Sloping Sides   This should measure 12 inches across the top and 10 inches across the bottom. These pans are usually made of aluminum and coated with Teflon. Imported enameled cast-iron pans with nonstick surfaces are also available. Attractive and useful as they are, they do, however, tend to be quite expensive.

Heavy 2-Quart Saucepan   Pans of enameled cast iron, stainless steel, or tin-lined heavy copper are all satisfactory.

Cookie Sheets   You will need two, preferably about 14 inches long and 18 inches wide. The best are those with slightly turned-up ends; the long sides of these, naturally, have no rims. Heavy cookie sheets are preferable to light ones because thin pans will sometimes warp or buckle disconcertingly during use.

Small Scissors   Any inexpensive scissors are satisfactory. In addition to other culinary uses, you will use them to cut notches or scallops around the pastry for pie shells and to make ornaments for top crusts.

Ruler   You will need a ruler, preferably one 15 to 18 inches long, to measure the diameter of your pastry.

Small Funnel   This will be used in the Deep-Dish Chicken Pie to prevent the filling from bubbling over.

Pastry Bag and Pastry Tips   These are fully described on page 88.

Plus—A Few of Your Basic Kitchen Utensils:

Measuring spoons
Flour sifter

Two sets of measuring cups
(one set for dry ingredients,
one set for liquids)
Pastry brushes
Sieves
Nutmeg grater
Rotary beater
Rubber spatulas
Bulb baster
Whisks
Wooden spoons

Not Necessary, But Helpful to Have

Pastry Board   Ideally, a pastry board should be large, certainly no smaller than 20 × 30 inches. It can be dispensed with if you have a large marble slab or a Formica counter top.

Pastry Cutters   One with a smooth cutting edge and another, called a jagger, with a jagged or serrated edge, are inexpensive and useful. The first will help you cut rounds or strips of dough with ease. The second will produce charming decorative strips for latticed pie tops.

Pie-Plate Holder   These attractive racks for holding a pie pan for table service may be made of bamboo, wicker, chromium, silver, or other metals.

Pie Server   A triangular-bladed spatula designed to cut and serve pie easily. Housewares departments have these in stainless steel or chromium. They are, of course, available in silver too.

Electric Mixer   A mixer with a pastry arm or paddle, such as the Kitchenaid mixers made by Hobart, is the most versatile.

American Apple Pie: A Model Double-Crusted Pie

The following recipe for apple pie is designed to serve as a model, as it were, for all double-crusted American pies. At first glance the recipe may appear to be unusually detailed, but I have structured it in this manner deliberately. After you make this apple pie, or the New England Clam Pie that follows it, you can securely take off on your own with any other double-crusted pie. If you already have a family favorite for a sweet or savory filling, mincemeat for example, use it, and follow the

same procedures for making and rolling the pastry, lining and filling the pan, adding and sealing the top crust, glazing and baking the pie. Whatever the filling, and incredible as it may seem, the baking time remains precisely the same.

A Few Words on Apples

Of all the apples that are found here in such colorful profusion, I much prefer Greenings to any other variety for my version of this classic American pie. If Greenings are unavailable, use any tart, crisp cooking variety; do not use such "eating apples" as McIntosh and Delicious—they are much too soft in texture and tend to fall apart when they are cooked.

American Apple Pie

Serves 6

THE FILLING:

2½ to 3 pounds of tart cooking
    apples, *or enough to make*
    7 cups of cubed apples
2 tablespoons butter
½ cup granulated sugar
½ cup light-brown sugar
½ teaspoon cinnamon
¼ teaspoon nutmeg,
    preferably freshly grated
2 to 4 tablespoons heavy cream
    (optional)

THE PASTRY:

2½ cups sifted all-purpose flour
1 teaspoon salt
1 cup chilled vegetable shortening
⅓ cup ice-cold water
¼ cup unsifted flour

THE COATING FOR THE LOWER CRUST:

2 teaspoons butter,
    softened at room temperature

THE GLAZE FOR THE TOP CRUST:

1 tablespoon milk

Making the Filling

Peel and quarter the apples and cut out the cores. Then cut each quarter into ½-inch cubes. (Cubes are, to my mind, preferable to slices because they retain their shape after cooking.) Don't attempt to make the cubes uniform in shape; the pieces need only be about the same size.

Over moderate heat, slowly melt 2 tablespoons of butter in a heavy 12-inch frying pan or skillet, preferably a Teflon-lined one. When the butter is completely melted but not brown, add the 7 cups of apples and sprinkle them with ½ cup of granulated sug-ar. Toss the mixture about with a rubber spatula to coat the apples evenly. Then, still over moderate heat, cook the apples for 2 or 3 minutes, turning them over continuously with the spatula until a slight film of liquid covers the bottom of the pan. Don't overcook the apples; they should barely have begun to soften.

Pour the contents of the frying pan into a large sieve set over a mixing bowl and let all the liquid drain through. Discard the juice, and transfer the drained apples to the mixing bowl.

Cool the apples to room temperature, or refrigerate them until you are ready to fill the pie.

Making the Pastry

To 2½ cups of sifted flour, add 1 teaspoon of salt and sift them together into a large mixing bowl. Add 1 cup of chilled shortening and toss the shortening about lightly to dust it with the flour.

With small chopping motions, use your pastry blender to cut through the shortening and distribute it throughout the flour. Run the blender around the bowl to incorporate any flour clinging to the sides and, occasionally, slide a table knife across the blender to free any shortening lodged in the wires. Continue to cut in the shortening until small (about rice-sized) pellets are formed. They needn't be uniform, so don't try to make them so.

Pour ⅓ cup of ice-cold water over the flour-shortening globules, and with a fork, toss them together lightly to make a moist crumbly dough. Quickly gather the mass together with your hands, then pat and shape it into a compact ball.

Hold the ball in one hand and, with the other, sprinkle it with ¼ cup unsifted flour, turning the ball about to flour it lightly and evenly.

Rolling the Dough

Cut the ball of dough in half and set one half aside. Place the other half on your floured pastry cloth and pat it into a circle about 4 inches in diameter.

Tips and Techniques . . .
Mixing tools

I will confess that cutting shortening into the flour and salt for my standard American pastry can be done with two knives instead of the pastry blender. But you will attain greater uniformity of texture if you use the pastry blender. A fork is the best utensil to use for mixing the fat-flour granules with the cold water.

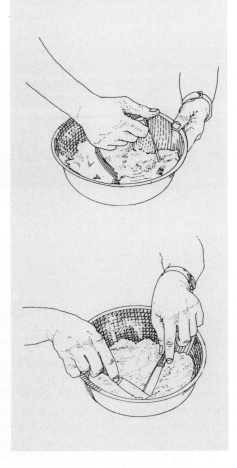

Position your rolling pin, encased in its floured sleeve, across the center of the dough and roll it away from you in one firm continuous stroke, lifting the pin as you near the edge.

Return the pin to the center of the dough, and, shifting your direction slightly to the right, again roll it away from you precisely as before.

1. Starting with your pin across center of the dough, roll outward from the center, never back and forth.

Continue this rolling procedure all around the circle, slightly overlapping each preceding stroke by about an inch. You will, after four or five strokes, reach a point where you must change your direction, rolling the dough toward rather than away from you. After a few such downward strokes you will find it necessary once more to change direction, again rolling the dough away from you until you complete the circle and reach the point where you began.

2. Lift the near edge of pastry and double it over rolling pin, which will roll away as you lift the pastry.

The finished rough circle of pastry should be about ⅛ inch thick and 14 inches in diameter. Measure it with your ruler to be sure. If the circle is too small, repeat the entire rolling process. Your finished 14-inch circle will probably be ragged around the edge, but don't be concerned. It will be trimmed later.

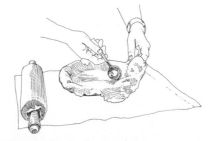

3. Unroll pastry from the pin over pie pan, allowing it to lie slackly across the pan. Never stretch pie pastry.

Lining the Pan

To avoid the precarious procedure of transferring the pastry to the pan with your hands, I prefer the easier (and safer) rolling-pin method.

Set the pin horizontally across the pastry about 4 inches away from the

4. Run the back of a teaspoon around sides of pan to fit the pastry snugly without stretching it.

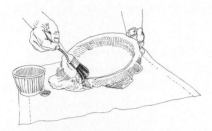

5. A coating of softened butter helps prevent sogginess of the bottom crust when filling is a moist one.

6. Unroll pastry for top crust over the filling in the same manner as lower crust was placed in pan.

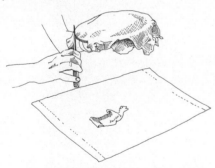

7. Trim overhanging edges of upper and lower crusts away together, using short strokes of a small sharp knife.

8. Make traditional crimped edge by pressing the tines of a fork into the pastry to seal the layers together.

edge closest to you. Now, using your fingers, lift the near edge of the pastry up and over the pin, guiding it away from you until it meets the other edge (the pin will move on its own). The rolling pin, its handles exposed, will now be enclosed in a half-moon of pastry, and you can securely proceed to line the pan.

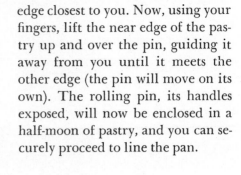

Tips and Techniques . . .
Flouring your pastry cloth
and rolling-pin sleeve

Before using a pastry cloth, rub enough flour into it to give the canvas a very smooth surface.

To flour the rolling-pin sleeve, slip it over your rolling pin and, with your hand, rub flour into it thoroughly before each use.

Always roll the pastry
in one direction, and on
one side only

Think of your circle of pastry as a clock, and the direction of your rolling strokes as the hand that goes around its face. To use a back-and-forth rolling motion, except when patching, will toughen pastry because it will overdevelop the gluten. For the same reason, it is unwise to turn pastry over and roll it on the other side.

Set your pie pan before you and, lifting the pin by its handles (use your thumbs to prevent the pastry from rolling off), hold the pin over the pan—not directly over the center, but rather a few inches beyond. Then lower the pastry, letting it fall slackly into the pan, bringing the pin toward you as you proceed. Ideally, the center of the pastry should be in the center of the pan.

To fit the slack pastry snugly into the crease of the pie pan, run the back of a teaspoon around it, using just enough pressure to mold the pastry without stretching it.

Coating the Lower Crust

Using a pastry brush, coat the bottom and sides of the pastry with the softened butter, spreading it as evenly as possible.

Preheating the Oven

Slide one of your oven shelves into the center slot of the oven, then set the thermostat at 450° and preheat the oven for 15 minutes.

Filling the Pie

Drain the apples once more and spread them evenly in the pastry-lined pan. In a small bowl combine ½ cup of brown sugar, ½ teaspoon of cinnamon, and ¼ teaspoon of nutmeg and stir them together with a

Tips and Techniques...
Decorating the top crust

If you have left-over pastry as well as the time and inclination to decorate your pie, gather the pastry scraps into a ball, roll them into a thin sheet, and use a small knife, scissors, pastry wheels, cookie cutters or any other instrument that occurs to you to cut the pastry into small designs of your choice. Leaves, triangles, flowers, and diamonds are all ornamental; or make any other shapes you fancy. Secure the pastry cutouts to the unbaked crust by brushing their undersides lightly with cold water or milk, then pressing them gently onto the crust.

fork, breaking up any lumps in the sugar. Sprinkle the mixture evenly over the apples.

Adding the Top Crust and Sealing the Pie

Roll out the reserved half of the dough precisely as you did the first half, but roll it only to a diameter of 11 inches.

With a pastry brush dipped into the tablespoonful of milk, lightly paint the lip of the lower crust (the pastry that lies over the flat rim of the pan), ignoring the overhanging edge.

Then lift the top-crust pastry onto your rolling pin as you did that for the bottom crust, and let it fall gently into place over the filling.

Hold the pan on the palm of your hand and, holding the flat of a small

Tips and Techniques . . .
To make a pie
with a fluted edge

Fluting is a more intricate technique for sealing edges than simply crimping them with a fork. It does, however, produce a charmingly decorative effect, and if you have the time, it is worth the effort.

After the pie has been filled, cover it with a top crust rolled out to a diameter of 12 to 13 inches. Then, with a pair of small scissors, trim both layers of overhanging pastry evenly about an inch beyond the rim of the pan.

Now lift the two layers of pastry, a small section at a time, and fold them under, thus making a four-layered edge resting on the flat rim of the pan.

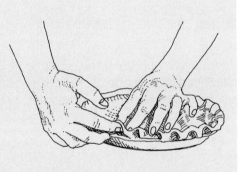

To make the fluting, spread the thumb and forefinger of one hand about an inch apart and set them lightly on the pastry rim. With the forefinger of your other hand push against the pastry on the rim as you pinch simultaneously with your left hand, thus forming an upstanding fluted ridge. Move all around the edge in this fashion. You may, if you like, go around a second time to deepen the fluting.

sharp knife pressed firmly against the rim, cut away the overhanging pastry with short slashing motions of the knife, rotating the pan slowly as you cut.

To seal the crusts together, set the pie down and press the back of the prongs of a table fork all around the rim. Don't press too firmly, or you may force the prongs through the pastry altogether.

Then cut a ¾-inch circle out of the center of the pastry to allow steam to escape as the pie bakes.

Glazing and Baking the Pie

Dip a pastry brush into the tablespoon of milk and brush the entire top surface of the pastry lightly and evenly.

Bake the pie for 10 minutes in the preheated 450° oven. Then lower the heat to 350° and bake the pie for 40 minutes longer, or until the crust is light golden brown and firm to the touch. Remove the pie from the oven and let it cool to lukewarm, or to room temperature, if you like, before serving it.

Serving the Pie

Just before you serve the pie you may, if you like, insert a small funnel or a plain pastry tip into the center opening of the pie and slowly pour into it the 2 tablespoons of cream (or use as much as 4 tablespoons if you like your pie really

Tips and Techniques . . .
Regulating the browning

Uneven browning occurs in some ovens, as pointed out under "How to Handle Hot Spots." The only way to cope with this problem is to observe your pie as it bakes. Even in my gas oven of the latest design, the back heats to a higher temperature than the front; so when I bake a pie, I check periodically on the browning of the crust. If one side seems to be browning more rapidly than the other (as alas, in my oven, it always does), I quickly turn the pale side around to the hotter area. If you must move or turn a pie, do it gently so as not to damage the crust, and do it quickly so that the oven door is not open long enough to cause the heat to lower appreciably. Moving or turning a pie will not hurt it a bit; for pies, unlike cakes, will not "fall" if shifted during baking.

You can cover the top of a pie loosely with aluminum foil if the crust appears to be browning too fast at any point.

moist). Then remove the funnel and slowly tilt the pie from side to side to distribute the cream evenly beneath the crust.

Alternatively, serve the pie with a pitcher of heavy cream, but I implore you, not with ice cream. Where this barbaric practice originated I don't know, but placing a scoop of ice cream on top of your pie will chill its delicate flaky crust to the texture of *papier-mâché*. If you *must* have ice cream with your pie, serve it in a separate dish.

New England Clam Pie

Serves 4 to 6

THE FILLING:

1½ cups drained minced clams
   (3 8-ounce cans) *or chopped*
   freshly shucked clams*
½ cup juice from the clams
3 eggs
½ cup cream
½ cup milk
¼ pound baked or boiled ham, *cut*
   into slivers about ½ inch long,
   ⅛ inch thick (about 1 cup)
½ cup coarsely crumbled crackers
   (preferably pilot crackers,
   but Uneeda Biscuits or
   unsalted Krispy Crackers
   are also suitable)
1 teaspoon strained
   fresh lemon juice
4 to 6 drops Tabasco
2 tablespoons finely
   chopped parsley
¼ teaspoon salt
Freshly ground black pepper
2 tablespoons butter

THE PASTRY:

2½ cups sifted all-purpose flour
1 teaspoon salt
1 cup chilled vegetable shortening
⅓ cup ice-cold water
¼ cup unsifted flour

THE COATING FOR THE LOWER CRUST:

2 teaspoons butter,
   softened at room temperature

THE GLAZE FOR THE TOP CRUST:

1 egg white
2 teaspoons water

If you are fortunate enough to find fresh clams they are, of course, preferable to canned ones. The number you will need to make 1½ cups of drained minced clams will naturally depend upon the size of the clams. Ordinarily, fresh clams, after shucking, are packed together with their liquid in a container. It is imperative that you drain the liquid through a fine sieve, preferably lined with cheesecloth, to rid it of all sand.

Making the Filling

Place the clams in a large strainer set over a mixing bowl and drain them thoroughly, shaking the strainer repeatedly to rid the clams of all possible juice. Pour ½ cup of the clam juice into a measuring cup and discard the rest.

Break 3 eggs into the same mixing bowl and, using a fork or a small whisk, beat them for a moment, or only long enough to combine the yolks and whites. Then stir in ½ cup of cream, ½ cup of milk, and the reserved ½ cup of clam juice. Stir gently until the ingredients are well combined. Add the drained clams, the cup of shredded ham, ½ cup of crumbled crackers, 1 teaspoon strained lemon juice, 4 drops Tabasco, 2 tablespoons chopped parsley, ¼ teaspoon salt and a liberal grinding of black pepper. Stir together thoroughly, then taste for seasoning.

Tips and Techniques . . . Coating the bottom crust

If a pie is to contain a moist filling, it is a good practice to brush the bottom crust with 1 or 2 teaspoons of softened butter before pouring in the filling. This will help to prevent sogginess, as will adding the filling at the last possible moment.

Tips and Techniques . . . Letting out the steam

All double-crusted pies must have openings of one kind or another in the top crust to release the steam formed by the filling as it cooks. In whatever shape you choose to cut them, always make these openings either in the center or as close to the center of the pie as you can. The filling is almost certain to boil over through openings made near the sides.

Add the extra drops of Tabasco and more salt and pepper if you think the filling needs it.

Refrigerate the filling while you make and roll out the pastry and line the pan.

Making the Pastry

Follow the directions in the recipe for American Apple Pie, page 18, for making and rolling the pastry, lining the pan, and coating the lower crust.

Preheating the Oven

Slide one of your oven shelves into the center slot of the oven, then set the thermostat at 450° and preheat the oven for 15 minutes.

Filling the Pie

Remove the filling from the refrigerator and stir it gently with a rubber spatula, then pour it into the pastry-lined pan. Use your spatula to spread out the solid ingredients, then dot the top evenly with 2 tablespoons of butter, cut into small bits.

Adding the Top Crust and Sealing the Pie

Follow the directions in the Apple Pie recipe for this procedure, using a pastry brush dipped into water to moisten the edges of the pastry before sealing them. Instead of cutting a circle out of the top crust, you may prefer to make two 1-inch slits close to the center of the pie.

Glazing and Baking the Pie

In a small bowl, using a whisk or a fork, beat the egg white with 2 teaspoons of water for a few seconds, or only long enough to combine them. Using a pastry brush, lightly coat the top crust with the mixture.

Bake the pie for 10 minutes in the preheated 450° oven. Then lower the heat to 350° and bake the pie for 40 minutes longer, or until the crust is light golden brown and firm to the touch.

Tips and Techniques . . .
Glazing the top crust

The top of a double-crusted pie may be given a better color and interesting highlights if it is brushed lightly with any one of the following glazes:

   cold milk
   light or heavy cream
   lightly beaten whole egg
   egg white, beaten
     for just a moment with
     2 teaspoons of cold
     water per egg white
   egg yolk mixed with two
     teaspoons of milk
     or cream.

Each glaze will give the surface a particular sheen, and it is really a matter of taste which of them you prefer.

I should note here that I disapprove of dusting the top of a pie with granulated sugar, as is often suggested. The sugar does indeed make the surface glitter, but the glitter is gained at the expense of toughening the crust.

Serving the Pie

Clam pie is equally good served warm or lukewarm; and, surprisingly, some New Englanders prefer it at room temperature, or even cold. I never serve it cold, and if I have any left-over pie, I reheat it in a preheated 325° oven for about 15 minutes, or until the crust and the filling are hot.

A Model Lattice-topped Pie

Although the lattice top gives this pie a charming and dramatic appearance, it is basically a double-crusted pie. There are numerous ways to make a lattice—some call for the skill of a weaver—but I prefer to keep the lattice simple because the final effect (and certainly the taste) is more or less the same. Like my American Apple Pie recipe, this one may be confidently used as a basic pattern for a pie containing any other filling.

Lattice-topped Cherry Pie

Serves 6

THE FILLING:
2 cans (1 pound each) pitted
  red sour cherries
  (3½ cups after draining)
1¼ cups juice drained from the
  cherries
½ teaspoon almond extract
1 cup sugar
3 tablespoons arrowroot
2 tablespoons coarsely
  chopped toasted almonds
  (available in cans)
1 tablespoon butter

THE PASTRY:
2½ cups sifted all-purpose flour
1 teaspoon salt
1 cup chilled vegetable shortening
⅓ cup ice-cold water
¼ cup unsifted flour

THE COATING FOR THE LOWER CRUST:
2 teaspoons butter,
  softened at room temperature

THE GLAZE FOR THE LATTICE:
1 tablespoon milk

Making the Filling

Pour the cherries and their juice into a large sieve set over a mixing bowl and drain them thoroughly, shaking the sieve from time to time. Then spread the cherries on a double layer of paper towels and gently pat them dry with more paper towels. Measure 1¼ cups of cherry juice and discard the rest.

Combine 1¼ cups of cherry juice, ½ teaspoon of almond extract, 1 cup

1. After lower crust has been filled, excess pastry is trimmed away to leave an overhang of half an inch.

2. Top-crust pastry has been rolled to 14-inch diameter. A pastry wheel is used to cut half-inch strips.

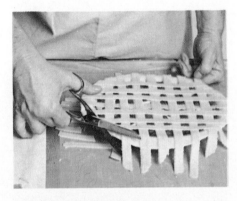

3. Strips and edge of crust have been brushed with milk. Strips laid half an inch apart form lattice.

4. Lattice completed, scissors are used to trim ends flush with the bottom-crust pastry overhang.

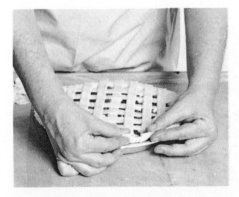

5. A small section at a time, layers of pastry are folded under to fit precisely on the lip of the pan.

6. Light pressure with tines of a fork seals pastry layers together all around edge before pie is baked.

of sugar, and 3 tablespoons of arrow-root in a heavy 2-quart saucepan. Stir them together briskly with a wire whisk and set the pan over moderate heat. Stirring constantly, bring the mixture to a boil, lower the heat and, still stirring, simmer it for 2 or 3 minutes, until it is smooth and thick. Add the drained cherries and remove the pan of filling from the heat.

Although you may allow the filling to cool in the pan if you wish, you can hasten the cooling by pouring the filling into a previously chilled bowl. However you do it, the filling should be at room temperature before you proceed.

Making the Pastry

Follow the directions in the recipe for American Apple Pie, page 18, for making and rolling the pastry, lining the pan, and coating the lower crust.

Preheating the Oven

Slide one of your oven shelves into the center slot of the oven, then set the thermostat at 450° and preheat the oven for 15 minutes.

Filling the Pie

Pour the cherry filling into the pastry-lined pan and spread the fruit out evenly with a rubber spatula. Sprinkle the 2 tablespoons of chopped toasted almonds over the top and dot with the tablespoon of butter, cut into small bits.

Making and Glazing the Lattice Top

With a small pair of scissors, cut away the excess pastry of the lower crust, leaving a uniform overhang of about ½ inch beyond the edge of the pan.

Roll out the other half of the dough precisely as for the first half. Using your ruler as a guide, cut the pastry with a small sharp knife or a plain or jagged pastry wheel into 18 strips half an inch wide.

Dip a pastry brush into the tablespoon of milk and coat the latticing strips lightly but evenly. Brush the rim of the filled lower crust with the milk. Carefully place one of the longest pastry strips horizontally across the center of the pie. Set another long strip over it vertically, thus forming a cross. Lay 4 more pastry strips about ½ inch apart on one side of the horizontal strip and 4 more on the other side, spacing them similarly. Form a lattice by laying the remaining strips in the opposite direction.

At first try, your finished lattice may lack the perfection you are aiming for, but with practice you will soon be able to achieve it. (In any case, I prefer the slightly irregular look of a homemade latticed pie to the machine-made appearance of a commercial baker's latticed top.)

Sealing the Pie

With your scissors, trim off the overhanging strips to make them match the ½-inch overhang of the bottom crust.

Now lift the bottom pastry and the overhanging strips together, a small section at a time, and fold them under to fit precisely on the lip of the pan.

To seal the layers together, press the prongs of a table fork all around the rim. Don't press too firmly at any point, lest you force the prongs through the pastry entirely.

Baking the Pie

Bake the pie for 10 minutes in the preheated 450° oven. Then lower the heat to 350° and bake it for 40 minutes longer, or until the lattice top is golden brown.

Remove the pie from the oven and let it cool to lukewarm or to room temperature before serving it.

Tips and Techniques ...
Protecting your oven
All fruit-filled pies have a tendency to bubble over as they bake. My cherry pie is no exception, although I have formulated the recipe in such a way as to minimize the possibility of this happening. As a safeguard against messing up your oven by such spillage, you might be wise to place a sheet of aluminum foil on the oven floor (but not on the rack upon which the pie is resting). Make sure that the foil doesn't cover any of the air vents, if yours is a gas oven; or that it lies flat without touching the heating element in an electric oven.

A Fully Baked, Scalloped Pie Shell

Making an unfilled, fully baked pie shell—which professionals often call a blind shell—is unquestionably a challenge. The tendency of the pastry to shrink in the pan as it bakes has driven even skillful cooks to the brink of despair. I think you will find my solution to this problem fascinating technically, and the results virtually foolproof. My American pie pastry, but naturally in reduced amounts, is used for this. You will no doubt notice the similarity of the directions for making and rolling the pastry to those in the model recipe for American Apple Pie, page 18. The

just enough pressure to mold the pastry without stretching it. Do not use your fingers to do this; a spoon is more effective.

Preheating the Oven

Slide one of your oven shelves into the center slot of the oven, then set the thermostat at 450° and preheat the oven for 15 minutes. During this period, continue with the construction of the shell.

Lining and Baking the Shell

Using a pastry brush and the 2 teaspoons of softened butter, coat a sheet of heavy-duty aluminum foil about 14 inches wide and 18 inches long.

Gently line the pastry-filled pan with the foil, buttered side down, fitting it closely to the pastry. (If you do not have wide foil on hand, use two narrower strips, overlapping them slightly.)

Fit a second 9-inch pie pan over the foil, allowing the excess foil to extend straight out all around between the doubled pans.

Holding the pans together, carefully turn them over and gently pat the pastry scallops out flat on the extended foil. Using a little pressure, push the upper pan down onto the lower one to enclose the pastry firmly.

Transfer this intricate-sounding—but in fact quite simple—construction to the preheated 450° oven, plac-

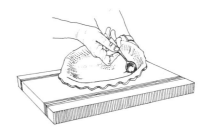

5. To fit pastry snugly to pan, run back of a teaspoon around the sides. Avoid stretching the pastry.

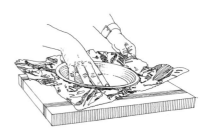

6. Fit a sheet of foil, buttered side down, into the pastry-lined pan. Add a second pan atop the foil.

7. Invert the construction, with pastry edge spread flat on foil. Place construction on oven shelf to bake.

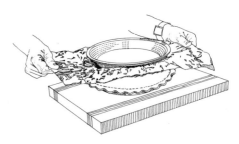

8. After cooling slightly, turn construction right side up and lift foil and inner pan from baked shell.

ing it directly on the shelf. Bake the shell undisturbed for 8 to 10 minutes, or until the exposed scalloped edge is golden brown.

Removing the Shell from the Oven

To take the baked shell out of the oven requires care to prevent the scalloped edge from breaking. Pull the oven shelf out and, with both hands holding the sides of the foil, slide the construction toward you. When the pan partially clears the shelf, slip your hand (protected by a potholder) under the pie pan and remove the shell—two pans, foil, and all—from the oven.

Place the construction on a table and let it cool for a few minutes for easier handling. Then turn the doubled pans right side up and, using the foil edges as handles, lift off the upper pan, exposing the pastry.

Cool the shell and fill it as directed in your recipe.

Tips and Techniques . . .
If a scalloped edge
should crumble

If by some mischance a scallop or two should crumble after you have baked a pie shell, simply cut away the remaining scallops with a small knife. Although this will destroy the decorative effect, the shell itself will be intact.

Tips and Techniques . . .
Freezing and keeping pastry

If you are a novice cook, it is wise to make at one time only the amount of pastry I specify for a single pie, because a small amount of dough is easier to manage than a large one.

With more experience, you can make a double amount and save the extra dough by wrapping it closely in foil and freezing it. It will keep in the deep-freeze for at least two months. Naturally, you will defrost the pastry before rolling it out.

You can also, if you like, roll out freshly made dough, line a pie plate, then seal the pan and the pastry in foil or freezer wrap and freeze it. Bake the crust in its frozen state, but increase the baking time somewhat.

Should you make your pastry in advance (not a bad idea), wrap it securely in plastic wrap and refrigerate it. Pastry may be kept in this state for at least two days, but before using it, let it soften at room temperature to a pliable state.

A pie shell with an extended scalloped edge lends distinction to Lemon Meringue Pie.

Lemon Meringue Pie — An Old Problem Solved

Even the most expertly made meringue—that favorite American topping of stiffly beaten egg whites and sugar, browned in the oven—almost inevitably produces an inordinate amount of liquid that collects over the filling and runs down into the bottom crust as the pie cools. This is called *weeping, and the term is apt.*

Until now, no foolproof way to control weeping has been generally known. Cream of tartar added to the egg whites supposedly does the trick, but in reality it doesn't. After count-

less experiments with a substance suggested by Dr. Paul Buck, of Cornell University, I have found that if I add to the egg whites, while beating them, a small amount of dicalcium phosphate and an equal amount of cream of tartar, the finished meringue will shed at most only a few tears.

Dicalcium phosphate is a nutritional supplement (it is included in some vitamin and mineral combinations) that is quite tasteless, and it does not affect the silky texture of the meringue in any way whatsoever.

If you can't find dicalcium phosphate powder in easily opened capsules at your drugstore, buy the tablets and crush them with a mortar and pestle or the back of a spoon. Dicalcium phosphate keeps indefinite-

ly and is inexpensive.

You might note here that whatever else you may have heard, there is little difference in volume and stiffness between egg whites at room temperature and those that are cold when you beat them.

Lemon Meringue Pie

Serves 6

THE PASTRY:

A Fully Baked, Scalloped Pie Shell,
  page 32

THE FILLING:

1 cup sugar
5 tablespoons cornstarch
¼ teaspoon salt
2 cups water
5 egg yolks
2 tablespoons very finely
  chopped lemon rind

2 tablespoons butter,
  cut into bits and
  softened at room temperature
⅓ cup strained fresh lemon juice
4 tablespoons finely crushed
  gingersnap crumbs

THE MERINGUE:

5 egg whites
¾ teaspoon cream of tartar

¾ teaspoon dicalcium phosphate
  (see introductory note above)
½ cup sugar

Making the Filling

In a heavy 2-quart saucepan, combine 1 cup of sugar, 5 tablespoons of cornstarch, ¼ teaspoon of salt, and 2 cups of water. Stir with a whisk until the sugar and cornstarch are dissolved, then cook over high heat, continuing to stir constantly, until the mixture comes to a boil and thickens. Lower the heat and con-

tinue to whisk for another 3 minutes, or until the mixture is very thick, shiny, and translucent. Remove the pan from the heat.

Then, one at a time, and working quickly, whisk the egg yolks into the mixture, making sure that each yolk has been thoroughly absorbed before adding the next one. Stir in 2 tablespoons of chopped lemon rind. Now cook the mixture over very low heat for 10 minutes, stirring constantly; don't let it boil. (To prevent it from boiling, lift the pan off the heat every 3 minutes or so to cool it slightly, then return it to the heat.)

If the mixture should become lumpy at any point, remove the pan from the heat, beat the filling vigorously until it is smooth again, then resume the cooking.

When the filling has cooked for the allotted 10 minutes, beat in the 2 tablespoons of butter, a few bits at a time. Then stir in ⅓ cup of lemon juice. Immediately pour the filling into another bowl and cool it until it is only slightly warm to the touch, whisking it now and then to keep it smooth.

Scatter the gingersnap crumbs evenly over the bottom of the baked pie shell and slowly pour in the still slightly warm filling, smoothing the top with a rubber spatula.

Refrigerate the pie for about 30 minutes, or until the filling is firm.

Preheating the Oven

Slide one of your oven shelves into an upper slot of the oven; then set the thermostat at 325° and preheat the oven for 15 minutes.

Making the Meringue

In a small, fine-meshed strainer set over a bowl, combine ½ cup of sugar, ¾ teaspoon of cream of tartar, and ¾ teaspoon of dicalcium phosphate; shake the strainer, stirring if you must to remove any lumps, until the mixture has been sieved into the bowl.

Using an electric mixer, a rotary beater, or a balloon whisk and copper bowl, beat the 5 egg whites briskly until they are thick and foamy. Then, still beating, add the sugar mixture a tablespoonful at a time. Continue to beat until the egg whites —now a meringue—are firm enough to hold stiff peaks on the beater when it is lifted and held up over the bowl. If you have any doubt about the consistency of the meringue, overbeat rather than underbeat it.

Now remove the pie from the refrigerator. With a rubber spatula, cover the entire surface of the filling with the meringue, making sure it extends ¼ inch over the rim of the pastry as well. Then, with your spatula, swoop small decorative peaks all over the surface of the meringue.

Baking the Meringue

Bake the pie in the preheated 325° oven for 20 to 25 minutes, or until the top of the meringue is a light golden brown with some marbling of white still showing.

Cool the pie to room temperature before serving it.*

Ideally, a lemon meringue pie should never be refrigerated. However, if the weather is very warm, you can refrigerate any left-over pie, but let it return to room temperature before serving it again.

It may come as a surprise to you that the pecan is indigenous to America, and that this sweet, smooth-shelled nut is closely related to the hickory nut. It grows in great profusion in the southern Mississippi valley, and anyone with a sweet tooth owes an enormous debt of gratitude to the creative Southern cook who made the first Pecan Pie.

Southern Pecan Pie   Serves 6 to 8

THE PASTRY:
A Fully Baked, Scalloped Pie Shell,
     page 32

THE FILLING:
2 cups dark corn syrup (a 16-ounce
     bottle of dark Karo syrup)
5 eggs
1 teaspoon vanilla

1 tablespoon butter
2 cups shelled pecan halves
     (a 6-ounce can)

THE TOPPING (OPTIONAL):
1 cup chilled heavy cream, *whipped*

Preheating the Oven

Slide one of your oven shelves into an upper slot of the oven; then set the thermostat at 325° and preheat the oven for 15 minutes. Meanwhile, make the filling for the fully baked pie shell.

Making the Filling

Pour 2 cups of dark corn syrup into a heavy 2-quart saucepan. Over high heat, bring the syrup to a turbulent boil. Then remove the pan from the heat.

Break 5 eggs into a medium-sized bowl and beat them with a whisk just until they are well combined but not foaming. Then, a tablespoonful at a time, pour 4 tablespoons of the hot syrup into the eggs, whisking well after each addition. Slowly pour the mixture, now slightly heated, in a thin stream into the pan of hot syrup, stirring constantly. Add the tablespoon of butter, cut into small bits. Continue to stir for 5 minutes, still off the heat; then add the teaspoon of vanilla.

Filling the Pie

Pull your oven shelf part way out and on it set the fully baked pie shell, still in its pan. Then, slowly and carefully, pour the hot filling into the shell. Sprinkle the 2 cups of pecan halves over the top, spreading them out evenly with a spoon or spatula.

Baking the Pie

Gently slide the shelf back into the preheated 325° oven and bake the pie for 30 to 40 minutes, or until the filling has browned slightly on top. Remove the pie from the oven (do this carefully, or the extended edge of the pastry may crumble).

Cool the pie to room temperature before serving it.

The Optional Topping

If you like to be traditional, serve the pie with a bowl of unsweetened whipped cream. Or spoon the whipped cream into a pastry bag fitted with a No. 9 star tip and pipe the cream around the edge of the pie in as fanciful a pattern as you wish.

Deep-Dish Fruit Pies

In traditional deep-dish pies, such as the Chicken Pie for which I give a recipe later, the filling and the top crust are baked at the same time; and this technique works very well indeed for a savory filling. However, deep-dish fruit pies made this way tend to bubble over, no matter how much care you exercise. Therefore, I have departed entirely from tradition for the deep-dish fruit pies that follow.

It is perhaps unorthodox to bake

the pastry first, cook the filling separately, and then combine the two. But the result is almost miraculous: the heat of the fruit seals the pre-baked lid to the filling, creating the illusion that the filling and pastry have been baked together—while you, the cook, are spared the unpleasant chore of cleaning the otherwise almost inevitably fruit-blackened, burnt oven.

I have devised these recipes with frozen fruit, so you need no longer wait for spring to make these delectable fruit pies. Because defrosting frozen fruit takes at least 2 hours, you may prefer to reverse the procedure in the two following recipes and defrost the fruit for the filling before you proceed to bake the pastry lid.

Deep-Dish Blueberry Pie

Serves 6

THE PASTRY:
1¼ cups sifted all-purpose flour
½ teaspoon salt
½ cup chilled vegetable shortening
3 tablespoons ice-cold water
2 tablespoons unsifted flour

THE GLAZE FOR THE CRUST:
1 tablespoon milk

THE FILLING:
3 packages (10 ounces each)
    frozen unsweetened blueberries
1 cup juice drained from
    the berries
¾ cup sugar
2 tablespoons cornstarch
2 tablespoons strained
    fresh lemon juice
½ teaspoon cinnamon

Making the Pastry

To 1¼ cups of sifted flour, add ½ teaspoon of salt and sift them together into a large mixing bowl. Add ½ cup of chilled vegetable shortening and toss it about lightly to dust it with the flour.

With small chopping motions, use your pastry blender to cut through the shortening and distribute it throughout the flour. Run the blender around the bowl to incorporate any flour clinging to the sides, and occasionally slide a table knife across the blender to free any shortening lodged in the wires. Continue to cut in the shortening until rice-sized globules are formed. They needn't be uniform, so don't try to make them so.

Pour 3 tablespoons of ice-cold water over the fat and flour granules and toss them together lightly with a fork to make a moist, crumbly dough. Quickly gather the mass together with your hands, then pat and shape it into a compact ball.

Hold the ball in one hand and, with the other, sprinkle it with 2 tablespoons of unsifted flour, turning the ball about to flour it lightly and evenly.

Rolling the Pastry

Place the ball of dough on your floured pastry cloth and pat it into a circle about 4 inches in diameter.

Position your rolling pin, in its

floured sleeve, across the center of the dough, and roll it away from you in one firm continuous stroke, lifting the pin as you near the edge.

Shifting your direction slightly to the right, return the pin to the center of the dough and again roll it away from you precisely as before.

Continue this rolling procedure all around the circle of dough, slightly overlapping each preceding stroke by about an inch. After four or five strokes you will reach a point where you must change direction, rolling the dough toward rather than away from you. And, after a similar number of downward strokes, you will find it again necessary to reverse direction; therefore, roll the dough away from you until you complete the circle and reach the point where you began.

The finished rough circle of pastry should be about 11 inches in diameter.

Preheating the Oven

Slide one of your oven shelves into the center slot of the oven, set the thermostat at 450° and preheat the oven for 15 minutes.

Making, Glazing, and Baking the Pastry Lid

Invert your 9-inch glass pie plate and place it directly in the center of the pastry circle. With a small sharp knife, cut through the pastry about

Tips and Techniques ...
To make individual
deep-dish fruit pies

If you prefer to make individual deep-dish pies in custard cups or other dishes of your choice, you can easily do so. Either the blueberry or the rhubarb filling will make:

4 individual pies in
   10-ounce custard cups, or
8 individual pies in
   5- or 6-ounce custard cups.

To make lids for individual pies, roll the pastry circle to a diameter of 15 or 16 inches, and use an inverted custard cup as a guide in cutting out the lids. Cut about ¼ inch outside the rim of the cup you use as a guide. Then prick, glaze, bake, and cool the lids in the same manner as outlined for the large deep-dish pie. The lids may require a moment or so less baking time because the pastry will probably be somewhat thinner than the single large pastry lid.

Tips and Techniques ...
**To decorate the lid
of a deep-dish pie**

Before baking a deep-dish pie lid, you can decorate it with a fanciful design, using a knife, fork, or cookie cutter to make such patterns as those illustrated.

¼ inch beyond the rim of the pie plate. Remove the plate and, with your hands or a large spatula, gently transfer the pastry to an ungreased cookie sheet. To prevent the pastry lid from puffing as it bakes, prick it all over with a fork; or decorate the lid with any pattern of perforations you like. (This will also prevent puffing.) Then brush the surface lightly with a pastry brush dipped in the milk.

Bake for about 10 minutes in the preheated 450° oven until the lid is light golden brown and feels firm to the touch. Slide it onto a wire cake rack to cool.

Making the Filling

Defrost the blueberries completely in a sieve set over a large bowl. Shake the sieve occasionally to drain the berries very thoroughly as they defrost. Measure the blueberry juice. It should come to 1 cup; if there is less, add water.

Tips and Techniques ...
**Never roll to the edge
of the pastry**

If you apply the pressure of your rolling pin all the way to the outer edge of the pastry circle, it will become brittle and thin. To avoid this, as you make each stroke you should lift your rolling pin off the pastry just before reaching the edge.

**If the pastry sticks
while you are rolling it**

If your pastry begins to stick to the sleeve or the pastry cloth, rub a little extra flour into the sleeve; or, if necessary, lift up the pastry and rub a little more flour into the cloth. Keep the amount of extra flour to a minimum; too much can toughen pastry.

In a heavy 12-inch frying pan, combine the blueberry juice with ¾ cup of sugar, 2 tablespoons of cornstarch, 2 tablespoons of lemon juice, and ½ teaspoon of cinnamon. Mix thoroughly.

Over moderate heat, bring the mixture to a boil, stirring it constantly with a whisk. Lower the heat and simmer it for about 2 minutes, or until it is thick and smooth. Then stir in the drained blueberries and simmer the mixture for 3 to 5 minutes, or until the berries are tender but still intact. Taste for sweetness—you may want to stir in a little more sugar.

Assembling and Serving the Pie

While the filling is still hot, scrape it into your 9-inch glass pie plate, using a rubber spatula. Then immediately—and carefully—lift up the baked pastry lid and place it over the filling.

Serve the pie while it is still warm. If it cools too much before serving time, set it in a preheated 325° oven and heat it for 10 minutes, making certain that the filling never comes to a boil or it will overspill disastrously and soil your oven.

Deep-Dish Rhubarb Pie

Except for the filling, this pie is made, assembled, and served in precisely the same way as the Deep-Dish Blueberry Pie in the preceding recipe. Other filling possibilities are described on page 45.

Deep-Dish Rhubarb Pie

Serves 6

THE PASTRY:
1 baked pie lid made
  as directed in the
  preceding recipe for
  Deep-Dish Blueberry Pie,
  page 41

THE FILLING:
2 packages (1 pound each)
  frozen unsweetened rhubarb
2 cups juice
  drained from the rhubarb
¾ cup sugar
2 tablespoons quick-
  cooking tapioca

Making the Filling

Defrost the frozen rhubarb completely in a sieve set over a large bowl. Transfer the drained rhubarb to a double thickness of paper towels and pat it dry with more paper toweling. Measure the rhubarb juice. It should come to 2 cups;

if there is less, add water to make up the amount.

In a heavy 12-inch frying pan, combine the 2 cups of rhubarb juice with ¾ cup of sugar and 2 tablespoons of tapioca. Mix them thoroughly. Add the rhubarb and let the mixture rest, uncovered, for 15 minutes.

Over moderate heat, bring the mixture to a boil. Lower the heat and simmer the rhubarb, stirring gently every now and then, for from 5 to 10 minutes, or until the sauce thickens lightly and the rhubarb is tender but not falling apart. (The tenderness of rhubarb varies a great deal—for that reason I have indicated so wide a range of cooking times.)

Assembling and Serving the Pie

As soon as the filling is done, pour it into your 9-inch glass pie plate and assemble and serve the pie as directed for Deep-Dish Blueberry Pie, page 41.

Tips and Techniques ...
To combine two fruits
in a deep-dish pie

There is no end to the variety of fruits you can combine for deep-dish fruit pies. If you like the combination of rhubarb and strawberries, add one 9- or 10-ounce package of frozen sliced strawberries, defrosted and drained, to the hot rhubarb filling after placing it in the pie dish. Or, add one small package of sliced frozen peaches, thoroughly defrosted and drained, to the hot blueberry filling in the pie dish before topping the pie with its baked pastry lid.

Deep-Dish Chicken Pie

Although this chicken pie is basically a traditional one—that is, the pastry and filling are baked at the same time—it departs from tradition in a significant way. It is unlike most chicken pies in that not one of the filling ingredients requires previous cooking. This results in a filling in which the essential flavor of each ingredient is retained to a remarkable degree. And as an added bonus, it is exceedingly simple to make.

Deep-Dish Chicken Pie
Serves 6

THE FILLING:

2 pounds chicken breasts,
  skinned, boned, and cut
  into ¾-inch cubes
2½ cups (about 2 pounds)
  baking potatoes, peeled
  and cut into ½-inch dice
1 cup (½ package) frozen peas,
  defrosted and drained
4 tablespoons finely
  chopped scallions
2 tablespoons canned pimientos,
  cut into small strips
2 tablespoons dried mushrooms,
  soaked in hot water for 15
  minutes, drained, then finely
  chopped; or finely chopped,
  drained, canned mushrooms
½ teaspoon dried leaf
  thyme, crumbled
½ teaspoon salt
Freshly ground black pepper
4 hard-cooked eggs,
  cooled, peeled, and cut
  in half lengthwise*

THE SAUCE:

4 tablespoons butter
5 tablespoons flour
1½ cups fresh or
  canned chicken broth
½ teaspoon salt
⅛ teaspoon strained fresh
  lemon juice

THE PASTRY:

1¼ cups sifted all-purpose flour
½ teaspoon salt
½ cup chilled vegetable shortening
3 tablespoons ice-cold water
2 tablespoons unsifted flour

THE GLAZE FOR THE CRUST:

1 egg yolk
2 teaspoons milk

Making the Filling

Place the chicken cubes in your 1½-quart soufflé dish. Add 2½ cups of diced potatoes, 1 cup of peas, 4 tablespoons of chopped scallions, 2 tablespoons of pimiento strips, 2 tablespoons of chopped mushrooms, ½ teaspoon of thyme, ½ teaspoon of salt, and a liberal grinding of black pepper. With either a wooden spoon or your hands, gently lift and toss the ingredients together. Set the dish aside while you prepare the sauce.

---

*To hard-cook eggs, let them come to room temperature and then lower them carefully, using a spoon, into a pan containing boiling water to cover them. Reduce the heat to low and simmer the eggs, uncovered, for 15 minutes. Plunge them into a bowl of cold water immediately, then either peel them immediately or let them cool first. Refrigerate the eggs until you are ready to use them.

Deep-Dish Chicken Pie. Only the eggs and the quickly made gravy are cooked before the pie goes into the oven.

Making the Sauce

In a heavy 2-quart saucepan, melt 4 tablespoons of butter, cut into bits, over low heat, being careful not to let it brown.

Remove the pan from the heat and stir in 5 tablespoons of flour to make a roux (as the mixture is called). Blend the butter and flour well, then pour in 1½ cups of chicken broth. With a whisk, beat the roux and stock together until they are well mixed.

Return the pan to high heat and, whisking constantly, bring the sauce to a boil. When the sauce is thick and smooth—a matter of a moment —lower the heat and simmer it for 2 or 3 minutes to rid it of any taste of raw flour.

Stir in ½ teaspoon of salt and ⅛ teaspoon of lemon juice. Taste for seasoning.

Pour the sauce over the ingredients in the baking dish. With a rubber spatula, gently lift and toss the chicken and other ingredients until they are thoroughly coated with the sauce.

Place the 8 halves of hard-cooked eggs over the filling, laying them, yolk side down and end to end, in a circle around the perimeter of the dish. The eggs should rise slightly higher than the top of the dish so that they will support the crust. Set the dish aside.

Preheating the Oven

Slide one of your oven shelves into a lower slot of the oven; set the thermostat at 450° and preheat the oven for 15 minutes.

Making and Rolling the Pastry

Follow the procedure in the recipe for Deep-Dish Blueberry Pie for making and rolling out the pastry. Roll it out to a diameter of 11 inches.

To trim the pastry, invert a 9-inch pie pan onto the rolled-out dough. With a small sharp knife or a plain pastry wheel, cut all around the pan, making a circle 10 inches in diameter. Remove the pan.

Topping, Sealing, and Glazing the Pie

Beat the egg yolk with the 2 teaspoons milk until they are just combined and, with a pastry brush, paint the rim of the filled soufflé dish, and paint a band 1½ inches wide around the outside of the dish below the rim.

Set your rolling pin horizontally across the pastry about 4 inches away from the edge closest to you. Now, with your fingers, lift the near edge of the pastry up and over the pin, guiding the pastry away from you until it meets the other edge (the pin will move on its own). The rolling pin, its handles exposed, will now be enclosed in a half-moon of pastry.

Lift the pin by its handles (use your thumbs to prevent the pastry from rolling off) and hold it over the dish—not over the center, but rather

Tips and Techniques . . .
Patching pastry

If pastry tears while you are rolling it, merely pull off a small piece from the edge, place it over the torn place, and firmly roll back and forth over it until the surface is smooth.

Stretching pastry

At no point when you are rolling out pastry or fitting it into a pan should you pull or stretch the dough. This will increase its elasticity and cause the pastry, like a rubber band, to retract to its original shape as it bakes.

a few inches beyond. Then lower the pastry, letting it fall gently over the filling and bringing the pin toward you until all the pastry has rolled off. Adjust the pastry over the dish, with a uniform overhang all around.

Double the overhanging pastry edge under itself and press it against the coated band on the dish to form a thick edge about 1 inch wide. Now, holding a table fork vertically, press the back of its prongs all around the band of pastry to secure the pastry to the dish.

Using a pastry brush, coat the crust evenly with the remaining glaze. Then, with a small sharp knife, cut a circle about ¾ inch in diameter in the center of the pastry, discard the cut-out disc, and insert a small funnel or a plain No. 9 pastry tip into the opening.

Baking and Serving the Pie

Bake the pie for 10 minutes in the preheated 450° oven, then lower the heat to 325° and continue baking it for 50 minutes more.

After the pie has baked for about 30 minutes, you will probably find that the sauce is bubbling up into the funnel or pastry tip in the center of the crust. If at any point the sauce threatens to bubble over, use a bulb baster to draw off the excess. Glance at the pie every 10 minutes or so for the rest of its baking time and repeat the removal of sauce whenever you think it necessary. (Save the gravy, if you like, and reheat it to serve with

Tips and Techniques...
Where to place pies
in the oven

Single-crusted pies are always to be placed on a shelf in the lower third of the oven, for the simple reason that the uncooked single crust requires the greatest amount of heat under it, not above it.

On the other hand, meringue-topped pies are always to be placed on a shelf in the upper third of the oven. Here, your intention is to brown the meringue quickly by the greater heat near the top of the oven. (The filling and the crust have been cooked beforehand.)

Always bake a double-crusted pie in the center of the oven because the pie bakes and browns more evenly when the heat is distributed equally around it.

the pie.)

The pie is done when its crust is a golden-flecked brown and firm to the touch.

Serve the pie at once.

A graham-cracker crust is a purely American concept, as are the crackers themselves, made from a flour invented by a Mr. Sylvester Graham. As for the chocolate mousse filling, it is indubitably French—and the combination produces a pie of great originality.

In making the crust for this pie, you need not be limited to graham-cracker crumbs: you may substitute finely crushed zwieback, gingersnaps, or vanilla wafers. And incidentally, my fully baked, scalloped pie shell (page 32) can be substituted for the crumb shell, if you like.

Chocolate Mousse Pie

Serves 6

THE CRUST:

1½ cups finely crushed
  graham-cracker crumbs
¼ cup sifted confectioners' sugar

1 teaspoon cinnamon
6 tablespoons butter,
  melted but not browned

THE FILLING:

½ pound semisweet chocolate
  (preferably Baker's),
  cut into small pieces;
  or ½ pound packaged
  semisweet chocolate bits
½ cup strong coffee, *or*
  1 tablespoon instant
  coffee powder, *dissolved*
  in ½ *cup boiling water*

1 teaspoon vanilla
2 egg yolks
2 egg whites
2 tablespoons sugar
½ cup chilled heavy cream

THE BORDER (OPTIONAL):

1 cup chilled heavy cream

Making the Crust

In a large bowl, combine 1½ cups of graham-cracker crumbs, ¼ cup of confectioners' sugar, and the teaspoon of cinnamon. With a wooden spoon stir them together thoroughly. Add 6 tablespoons of melted butter and mix the ingredients until the butter is completely absorbed.

Then dump the mixture into a 9-inch aluminum pie pan and, using your fingers, press and pat it as evenly as possible over the bottom and up the sides of the pan.

Set a second 9-inch pie pan into the crumb-lined one and press it

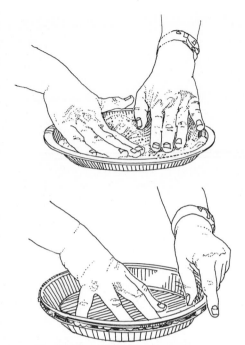

down firmly. Remove the upper pan and, if any further shaping of the crust is necessary (this will be likely only around the sides), press any uneven spots smooth with your fingers.

To firm the crust, refrigerate the shell for at least 2 hours before filling it. *This is absolutely essential.*

Making the Filling

Place ½ pound of semisweet chocolate in the top of a double boiler, add ½ cup of coffee, and fit the top into the lower section, which has been partially filled with hot water.

Set the boiler over moderate heat and stir the chocolate and coffee together constantly with a rubber spatula until the chocolate melts and the mixture is smooth. Then take the double boiler off the heat and re-

move the upper pan. Stir 1 teaspoon of vanilla into the chocolate mixture and set it aside to cool slightly—for not more than 2 minutes—stirring it once or twice.

Now, with a whisk, beat the 2 egg yolks into the chocolate mixture one at a time, continuing to beat until the yolks are completely absorbed. Set the filling aside to cool to room temperature.

Beat 2 egg whites with a rotary or electric beater, or in a copper bowl with a balloon whisk, until they are thick and foamy; add 2 tablespoons of sugar and continue beating rapidly, moving the beater around the bowl as you beat, until the whites form very firm, unwavering peaks on the beater when it is lifted.

Beat ½ cup of cream in another bowl—preferably a chilled one—using the same beater without bothering to wash it. The cream should not be stiff—beat it only until it will form soft peaks.

With a rubber spatula, gently stir the beaten whites into the whipped cream, keeping the mixture as airy as possible. Then thoroughly stir 2 tablespoons of the combination into the chocolate mixture to lighten it.

Using your spatula, scrape the chocolate mixture over the combined egg whites and cream. Still using the spatula, gently fold the mixtures together, combining the two by cutting down through both and lifting the heavier mass over the lighter, just until no streaks of white show. Do not overmix, or the mousse will be heavy.

Chilling the Pie

Pour the mousse into the pie shell, spreading it out evenly with your spatula. Refrigerate the pie for at least an hour to allow the mousse to become firm.*

---

*Like all desserts containing cream, the pie should be kept refrigerated until serving time.

Making the Border (Optional)

If you wish to decorate the pie, whip the cup of chilled heavy cream until it will form firm but still slightly wavering peaks. Following the illustrations on page 95, spoon the whipped cream into a pastry bag fitted with a No. 9 star tip. Pipe the cream around the edge of the pie in as fanciful a pattern as you wish.

Orange-Apricot Chiffon Pie

Serves 6 to 8

THE CRUST:

A chilled 9-inch crumb crust made as in preceding recipe for Chocolate Mousse Pie; or a

Fully Baked, Scalloped Pie Shell, page 32

- -

THE FILLING:

1 envelope unflavored gelatin
½ cup water
4 egg yolks
4 tablespoons sugar
½ cup strained fresh orange juice
1 tablespoon orange rind, *finely chopped*

⅛ teaspoon salt
2 cans (1 pound, 1 ounce each) pitted apricots, *drained and rubbed through a medium-fine sieve* (about 1½ cups pulp)
4 egg whites

- -

THE GARNISH (OPTIONAL):

1 small can mandarin oranges, *thoroughly drained and patted dry with paper towels*

½ cup chilled heavy cream, *stiffly whipped*

Making the Filling

Sprinkle the gelatin into a glass measuring cup containing ½ cup of cold water. Set aside and allow the gelatin to soften for about 5 minutes.

In the top pan of your double

boiler, off the heat, beat 4 egg yolks for 2 minutes with a whisk, then beat in 2 tablespoons of the sugar, continuing to beat for about 2 minutes more, or until the mixture is thick enough to run sluggishly off the beater in a ribbon when it is lifted out of the pan. Now stir in ½ cup of orange juice, the tablespoon of chopped orange rind, and ⅛ teaspoon of salt.

Insert the top pan into the lower pan, which has been partially filled with hot water. Set the double boiler over moderate heat. With a rubber spatula, stir the mixture for about 5 minutes, or until it becomes smooth and fairly thick; or in other words, a custard.

Add the softened gelatin to the custard and stir for about 30 seconds to dissolve the gelatin completely. Scrape the mixture into a large bowl and thoroughly stir in the apricot purée.

Refrigerate for about ½ hour, only until the mixture thickens to a pudding-like consistency. Check it from time to time. If it should become lumpy at any point, beat it briskly with a whisk until smooth, then complete the chilling.

With a rotary or electric beater, or using a copper bowl and a balloon whisk, beat 4 egg whites for a minute or two, just until foamy. Then add the remaining 2 tablespoons of sugar and continue beating rapidly, moving the beater around the bowl from time to time as you beat, until the whites form firm but slightly wavering peaks when the beater is lifted

out of the bowl. If in doubt, underbeat rather than overbeat. Overbeaten egg whites will make the filling spongy rather than velvety.

Mix 2 heaping tablespoons of the beaten whites into the apricot mixture, then, with a rubber spatula, scrape the mixture over the remaining whites in the bowl. Slowly and gently fold the two together, constantly cutting down and lifting the heavier mass over the lighter mass and running the spatula around the sides of the bowl occasionally. Do not overfold; stop when traces of egg whites no longer show.

Filling and Serving the Pie

Pour the filling into the chilled pie shell, mounding it slightly in the center, and smoothing the surface with a spatula as evenly as you can.

Refrigerate the pie for at least an hour, or until the filling is firm. The pie can remain in the refrigerator for as long as 6 hours before you serve it. It will inevitably sink a bit as it chills, but this will have no effect whatsoever on its light texture.

The Optional Garnish

You may, if you like, garnish the chilled pie with overlapping slices of mandarin oranges, laid in a ring around the outer edge. To gild the lily further, you might mound the whipped cream in the center just before serving the pie.

Tarts in several guises: Cheese Tartlets, to accompany drinks; Swiss Potato and Sausage Tart, a savory main dish; and a classic strawberry-topped dessert tart.

Tarts and Tartlets—A Franco-American Alliance

There is an essential difference, theoretically at least, between a French tart and an American pie. A tart is a filled pastry shell, open-faced, which is usually removed from its pan before it is served. A pie, on the other hand, is generally thought of as a filled pastry, usually with both a top and a bottom crust, but sometimes with only one or the other. A pie is, of necessity, always left in its pan, but for serving it may be placed in a holder made of anything from wicker to sterling silver.

With the passage of years the two culinary categories have overlapped. Although the American pie has rather brazenly taken on some of the characteristics of the French tart, both tarts and tartlets (small individual tarts) have, in some mysterious fashion, retained their original identity. Undoubtedly the French, always rigid classicists when it comes to culinary matters, are responsible for this; they wouldn't dream of concealing their symmetrically patterned fruit fillings, or the quivering, delicate savory custards they call *quiches*. And of course they are right. Why, as a French cook might sensibly ask, should an exquisite filling be asked to play a minor role in a magnificent production instead of being its star, with its colors and patterns clearly visible?

Utensils You Will Need for Tarts and Tartlets . . .

Tart Pans   One or two fluted, loose-bottomed tart pans, 9 inches in diameter and 1 inch deep, will be needed. Imported from France or Germany, the tart pans are usually inexpensive and are available in shops that specialize in cooking equipment, or in housewares departments, or by mail order. Check the size of the pan by measuring it directly across the bottom. Your so-called 9-inch pan may turn out to be from ¼ inch to 1 inch larger or smaller. My tart recipes are designed to fill a 9-inch shell to the brim.

Small Muffin Pans   Two 12-cup muffin pans, with cups ¾ inch deep and measuring 2 inches across the top, will be needed for tartlets. These pans are most satisfactory when they are Teflon-lined because the lining makes the removal of the tartlets (to say nothing of clean-up) so simple.

3-Inch Cookie or Biscuit Cutter   The cutter can be either plain or fluted; it will be used for cutting out pastry for tartlets.

Wire Cake Racks   Two racks, each 10 × 14 inches, will be most useful. They are inexpensive, and need not be particularly heavy.

Plus—The same rolling pin, pastry blender, pastry cloth and rolling-pin sleeve, mixing bowls, ruler, and heavy 2-quart saucepan that you need for pies, all listed in the preceding section.

And a Few of Your Basic Kitchen Utensils:

Two sets of measuring cups
   (one set for dry ingredients,
   one set for liquids)
Measuring spoons

Flour sifter
Pastry brushes
Sieves
Nutmeg grater
Wooden spoons
Rubber spatulas
Whisks
4-sided grater

Rotary beater

Not Necessary, But Helpful to Have

Pastry Board   This board, also helpful to have in making pies, is described on page 17.

Tart Pastry

The pastry I use for tarts is a version of the classic *pâte brisée,* a French short pastry. It is somewhat richer and less flaky than American pastry and contains a considerable amount of butter in addition to shortening. Although it takes some practice to roll out, the result is worth the effort. The tart shells—at least those in this book—are always baked before they are filled.

You might note, by the way, that the recipe for tart pastry makes more than enough dough to line the 9-inch tart pan. I find that this is an advantage for novice cooks because it gives them an embarrassment of riches, as it were, to play around and experiment with; and any left-over pastry can be frozen. An experienced cook may choose to make half the amount of pastry I call for, or to make two tart shells from the original recipe. But whether you are experienced or not I would suggest that, at least the first time, you make the dough in the quantity I indicate.

And you will also want to note that it is essential to chill this dough; so make it well ahead of time.

A Fully Baked, Fluted Tart Shell

Makes a fully baked, unfilled 9-inch shell

2 cups sifted all-purpose flour
½ teaspoon salt
8 tablespoons butter
   (a quarter-pound stick),
   *cut into ¼-inch pieces
   and thoroughly chilled*
3 tablespoons shortening,
   thoroughly chilled
⅓ cup ice-cold water
¼ cup unsifted flour

**FOR COATING THE TART PAN
   AND THE LINING FOIL:**
2 teaspoons butter,
   softened at room temperature

Tips and Techniques ...
Chilling the ingredients

To be sure that any ingre-
dients that should be chilled
will be at the correct temper-
ature, read the recipe completely before you begin.
This is simple-sounding ad-
vice, but disasters (minor
ones, at least) can follow if
you don't heed it.

Because of its considera-
ble butter content, my
French tart pastry tends to
soften as you rub the fats
with the flour. As the blend-
ed mixture should be dry
and mealy or flaky rather
than oily, it is necessary that
the butter, shortening, and
water (and even the flour and
the bowl, if you are a perfec-
tionist) be extremely cold
when you begin to work.
This chilling will counteract
the effect of the warmth of
your fingers.

and fats together, using the thumbs
and first two fingers of each hand in
a sliding motion—as if you were
counting out money. Do not squeeze
or press the dough.

After a moment or two, interrupt
this manipulation by cupping a
handful of the mixture in your
hands and rubbing them together
with a sliding motion, letting the
flakes fall into the bowl. Then return to the thumb-and-finger operation. These alternating procedures
will aerate the mixture and prevent
it from becoming oily. Continue until the fats and flour are fairly well
integrated in comparatively dry
flakes. Don't attempt to make the

Making the Pastry

To 2 cups of sifted flour add ½
teaspoon of salt and sift them together into a large mixing bowl.
Add 8 tablespoons of butter and 3
tablespoons of shortening. Toss the
ingredients together with your
hands to coat the butter and shortening with flour. Then rub the flour

blend too uniform; there should be occasional small nuggets of flour-coated fat among the blended flakes.

Immediately pour ⅓ cup of ice-cold water over the mixture and toss it with your hands until you are able to gather the dough into a compact ball. If for any reason it seems crumbly (most unlikely), sprinkle in an additional teaspoon, no more, of cold water. You should then have no difficulty in patting the dough into

> ### Tips and Techniques ...
> ### Mixing methods
> *Do not use your pastry blender to mix French tart pastry. The texture you are aiming for can be achieved only by rubbing the flour, the butter, and the shortening together with your fingers to form a fat-flour structure that is quite different from that of American pie crust: the aim is to rub the ingredients into flakes consisting of blended flour and fat. This structure of the un-baked dough is the key to the correct texture.*
>
> *For mixing tartlet pastry, however, I find a blender more effective than fingers because the object is to achieve a fine granular texture. You may, however, use your fingers if you like.*

> ### Tips and Techniques ...
> ### The importance of making the pastry ahead of time
> *Plan to make the tart pastry and refrigerate it for 3 hours, or even a day, before you will use it. The success of this rich pastry depends in large measure upon having all the ingredients thoroughly chilled and upon combining the chilled ingredients speedily.*

a ball.

Hold the ball of dough in one hand and, with the other, sprinkle it with ¼ cup of unsifted flour, turning the ball about to flour it lightly and evenly.

Chilling the Dough

Wrap the dough in plastic wrap or put it into a plastic bag and refrigerate it for at least 3 hours, or for a day, or even overnight. This pastry must be thoroughly chilled before it is used.

Rolling the Dough

Remove the dough from the refrigerator, unwrap it, and let it rest at room temperature until it softens just enough for you to press your forefinger into it fairly easily. Don't

The French traditionally roll their pastry on a hardwood board or a marble slab. You can follow their practice if you wish, but you will have a considerably easier time of it if you use a pastry cloth and a stockinette sleeve for your rolling pin, as in making American pie crust.

find it again necessary to reverse direction; so roll the dough away from you until you complete the circle and reach the point where you began. When you finish, you should have a rough circle about ⅛ inch thick and about 13 inches in diameter. If the circle is too small, repeat the entire rolling process.

Set the rolling pin horizontally across the pastry about 4 inches away from the edge closest to you. Now, with your fingers, lift the near edge of the pastry up and over the pin, guiding the pastry away from you until it meets the other edge (the pin will move on its own). The rolling pin, its handles exposed, will now be enclosed in a half-moon of pastry.

Lining the Tart Pan

let the dough get too soft.

Place the ball of dough on your floured pastry cloth and pat it into a circle about 4 inches in diameter.

Position your rolling pin, in its floured sleeve, across the center of the dough and roll it away from you in one firm continuous stroke, lifting the pin as you near the edge.

Shifting your direction slightly to the right, return the pin to the center of the dough, and again roll it away from you precisely as before. Continue this rolling procedure all around the circle of dough, each time overlapping the last stroke by about an inch. You will, after four or five strokes, reach a point where you must change your direction, rolling the dough toward rather than away from you. After a similar number of downward strokes you will

With your pastry brush and 1 teaspoon of the softened butter, coat the entire inside surface of your tart pan.

Lift the rolling pin by its handles (use your thumbs to prevent the pastry from rolling off) and hold the pastry-laden pin over the tart pan—not over the center, but rather a few inches beyond. Then lower the pastry, letting it fall slackly into the pan, bringing the pin toward you until all the pastry has rolled off.

Although the pastry will now cover the pan, it will not be fitted into it fully. To achieve this, gently lift up a small section of the overhanging edge with your fingers and let the pastry fall slackly into the crease

Tips and Techniques—The French Way

To roll dough on a pastry board, marble slab, or Formica surface

Spread 2 tablespoons or so of unsifted flour on your pastry board, Formica-topped counter, or marble slab. Place the dough on the surface and pat it lightly into a circle about 4 inches in diameter. If it tends to crack or seems unmanageable, it is still too cold; let it soften before proceeding.

Now dust a little flour over the dough, and starting at the center, roll the pin away from you in one continuous stroke, lifting the pin before you reach the edge exactly as in rolling dough on a pastry cloth. However, after each stroke, gently turn the entire circle an inch or two to the right and sprinkle a little more flour under it if it seems to be sticking. Continue to roll from the center, turning the dough an inch to the right after each rolling, and dusting a little flour under and over it whenever you think it necessary. When you finish, you should have a rough circle about ⅛ inch thick and 12 to 13 inches in diameter. If the circle is too small, repeat the entire rolling and rotating process until it is large enough.

Flan rings

For centuries French tarts (or flans, as they are also called —not to be confused with Spanish flans, which are custards) were—and still often are—shaped and baked inside flan rings, metal hoops that are set on a baking sheet, lined with pastry, and baked unfilled (or blind, in culinary terms).

Once the shell has been prebaked the ring is removed, the pastry shell is filled, and the whole is then baked again.

In my opinion, fine French cookbooks to the contrary, the use of a flan ring requires the virtuosity of a professional pastry maker; and even some professionals (as a few have admitted to me) have trouble with them. Quite commonly the pastry will slump unattractively, and breaking the shell is a constant danger. A far better and more reliable alternative to the flan ring is the fluted, loose-bottomed tart pan.

Tips and Techniques ...
Gluten and the
stretching of dough

French tart pastry will re-
act precisely like flaky pastry
—such as my American pas-
try—if you overmix it or re-
roll it or stretch it excessive-
ly. Like pie pastry, the tart
and tartlet pastries should be
eased into the pan without
any stretching at all—they
should lie in the pan in a
thoroughly relaxed way.

of the pan. Continue to do this, section by section, until the pan is lined
with pastry lying slackly in place.
Then, using a fingertip, gently press
the pastry into each fluting of the
side of the pan until it fits snugly all
around. To form a more definite
crease, run the back of a teaspoon all
around the pastry where the flutes

meet the bottom of the pan.

To remove the overhanging pastry, run your rolling pin across the
top of the tart pan. The excess pastry will fall away, leaving a perfectly
smooth edge.

You may bake the shell at once; or
refrigerate the pastry-lined pan until
you are ready to use it.

1. Turn the pin slowly toward you to allow
the tart pastry to fall slackly into and across
the pan.

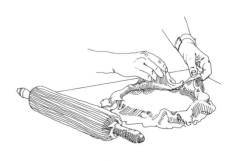

2. Lift a small section of pastry at a time
and coax it into place around the sides of
pan.

3. Using a fingertip, press the pastry gently
into the flutings of the pan until it fits
snugly all around.

4. With the back of a spoon, form a definite
crease all around the pastry where the flutings meet the bottom.

Preheating the Oven

Slide one of your oven shelves into the middle slot of the oven; set the thermostat at 425° and preheat the oven for 15 minutes.

Baking the Tart Shell

Cut a sheet of 12- or 14-inch aluminum foil 24 inches long, double it, and brush one side evenly with the remaining teaspoon of softened butter, using a pastry brush. Place the foil, buttered side down, across the pan, and press it very gently down and into the crease to support the sides of the pastry as it bakes.

Pour in about a cupful of small dry beans (or even pebbles will do) and spread them evenly on top of the foil.

Bake the shell in the preheated 425° oven for 10 to 12 minutes, or until you see the rim of the pastry beginning to turn a very pale brown. Then, using both hands, lift out the foil holding the beans.

To prevent the pastry from puffing as baking is completed, prick the bottom of the crust lightly all over its surface, using a table fork. Don't, however, pierce the pastry so deeply that you break entirely through.

Reduce the oven temperature to 375° and bake the shell about 8 minutes longer, or until it is golden brown and firm to the touch. I suggest that you check the shell after

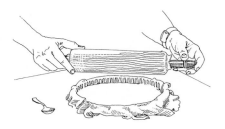

5. Run the rolling pin firmly over the rim of pan to cut away excess pastry, leaving a flush edge.

6. Fit doubled foil, buttered side down, into shell, then weight it down with beans or pebbles.

7. After 10 to 12 minutes' preliminary baking, remove the foil and beans. Beans may be used again.

8. Prick shell lightly all over bottom to prevent blistering during final 8-minute baking period.

about 5 minutes of this final period, because oven temperatures can depart from the thermostat settings and the shell may be baking faster than you think.

Let the shell cool in its pan.

Tips and Techniques . . .
Repairing a broken
tart shell

You may occasionally find, if you are careless or hurried, that the edge of the baked pastry shell has crumbled or broken enough to make it impossible to fill the shell. There is a simple way to line the shell so that it will hold the filling without leakage while it bakes.

Following the sketches, build a new edge with a strip of buttered aluminum foil. This damming device is particularly useful when the shell is to be filled with custard; it will serve to contain the liquid custard, and when the filling is fully cooked the strip can be removed.

To make a foil "dam" for a broken edge, butter a foil strip wider and longer than the break.

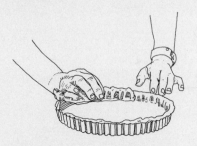

Press buttered side of foil against flutings and the bottom. Fill and bake tart; remove foil.

A Partially Baked, Fluted Tart Shell

Makes a 9-inch shell

Make the pastry exactly as described in the preceding recipe and bake the shell for the first period (10 to 12 minutes). After removing the foil and beans and pricking the surface of the pastry, lower the heat to 325° and reduce the second baking time to about 3 minutes. When the partially baked shell has barely begun to brown, remove it from the oven. Let the shell cool in its pan before filling it.

This is essentially a version of the French quiche Lorraine, *except that it uses ham and cheese instead of cheese alone. You may, if you like,* substitute for the ham the same quantity of another meat, such as cooked tongue or fried bacon, with interesting effect.

Ham and Cheese Tart   Serves 6

THE PASTRY:
A Fully Baked, Fluted Tart Shell,
    page 57

- -

THE FILLING:

¼ pound baked or boiled ham,
    trimmed of all fat and
    cut into ¼-inch to ½-inch
    cubes (about 1 cup cubed ham)
2 eggs
¾ cup milk
¼ cup heavy cream
¾ teaspoon salt

Freshly ground black pepper
½ teaspoon dry mustard
⅓ cup freshly grated imported
    Parmesan cheese,
    plus 2 tablespoons
    to be used for topping
1 tablespoon butter

- -

THE GARNISH:
1 tablespoon finely chopped parsley

Preheating the Oven

Slide one of your oven shelves into an upper slot of the oven; set the thermostat at 325° and preheat the oven for 15 minutes.

Making the Filling

For the custard, break 2 eggs into a 2-quart mixing bowl and, with a

Tips and Techniques . . .
A reminder about butter
I always make my tart and tartlet pastries with sweet (unsalted) butter. If you prefer to use salt butter, reduce the amount of salt called for in the recipe by one half.

fork or a small whisk, beat them for a few seconds, or only long enough to combine them. Then stir in ¾ cup of milk, ¼ cup of cream, ¾ teaspoon of salt, a liberal grinding of black pepper, ½ teaspoon of dry mustard, and ⅓ cup of grated Parmesan cheese. Stir gently until the ingredients are well combined. Taste for seasoning; the custard mixture may need more salt and pepper.

Filling the Tart

Spread the cup of cubed ham in the baked tart shell.

Pull the upper oven shelf forward and place the baked shell on it.

Tips and Techniques ... Baking temperatures

Tart shells are always baked in the center of the oven and at a fairly high temperature. After filling, however, the tart is set on an upper shelf so that the heat will be greater above the filling than below the previously baked crust. Custard fillings are baked at a lower temperature than others in order to prevent them from curdling.

If your oven has "hot spots," you may safely move any tart around to avoid uneven baking.

Tips and Techniques ... If your pastry should tear

If the pastry should tear while you are rolling it—and alas, it often does—merely cut a small piece from the edge, brush it lightly with water, and patch it into place, moistened side down, over the opening. Dust it with a little flour and roll your pin back and forth over it until the surface is smooth again. Do not use this back-and-forth motion in rolling except when you are patching—it would toughen the pastry—and never, for any reason, turn the dough over and roll the underside.

Then pour the custard mixture into the shell. If the filling threatens to overflow the rim (the pastry may have contracted a bit too much during baking), stop pouring and discard the surplus custard.

Sprinkle the extra 2 tablespoons of grated Parmesan cheese over the filling and dot it evenly with the tablespoon of butter, cut into bits.

Baking the Tart

Gently slide the laden shelf back into the preheated 325° oven and bake the tart for about 30 minutes, or until the custard is firm and a small table knife inserted into its center emerges almost, but not entirely, dry.

Serving the Tart

Remove the tart from the oven and set it on top of a tall coffee can or any object of similar shape, carefully holding onto the sides of the pan. Check to see if the fluted sides of the pan will separate easily from the baked shell — if the filling has cooked over at any point, the pastry may adhere to the metal. Free any such areas with the point of a small knife before gently guiding the outer rim down to the table top.

Slide the tart, still on its metal base, onto a serving platter. Sprinkle the tart with the tablespoon of chopped parsley and serve it at once; or cool it to lukewarm, if you prefer.

Crabmeat Tart

Cooked lobster or cooked shrimp, shredded or chopped, may be substituted for the crabmeat in this tart with equal success.

If you use lobster, you might replace the chives by 1 tablespoon of chopped fresh tarragon; with the shrimp, you might use 2 tablespoons of chopped fresh dill.

These three herbs are interchangeable in any version of this tart, depending upon your taste or the fresh herbs you may have on hand. Do not use dried herbs, however. Frozen chopped chives are acceptable in place of fresh chives. Lacking all else, use fresh parsley, which is always available.

Crabmeat Tart

Serves 6

THE PASTRY:
A Fully Baked, Fluted Tart Shell, page 57

THE FILLING:
1 cup fresh-cooked crabmeat *or a 6½-ounce can of crabmeat, thoroughly drained; or 1 cup frozen crabmeat, defrosted and thoroughly drained*
2 eggs
¾ cup milk
¼ cup heavy cream

¾ teaspoon salt
⅛ teaspoon white pepper
2 tablespoons finely cut fresh chives *or 3 tablespoons frozen chopped chives*
2 tablespoons freshly grated imported Parmesan cheese
1 tablespoon butter

Preheating the Oven

Slide one of your oven shelves into an upper slot of the oven; set the thermostat at 325° and preheat the oven for 15 minutes.

Making the Filling

Remove and discard any bits of shell or cartilage from the crabmeat. Then, using your fingers, shred the meat coarsely.

For the custard, break 2 eggs into a 2-quart mixing bowl and, using a fork or a small whisk, beat them for a few seconds, or only long enough to combine them. Then stir in ¾ cup of milk, ¼ cup of cream, ¾ teaspoon of salt, ⅛ teaspoon of white pepper, and 2 tablespoons of finely cut fresh chives or 3 tablespoons of frozen chopped chives. Stir gently until the ingredients are well combined. Taste for seasoning; the mixture may need more salt and pepper.

Filling the Tart

Scatter the shredded crabmeat evenly in the baked shell.

Pull the upper oven shelf forward and place the baked shell on it. Then pour in the custard mixture. If the filling threatens to overflow (the pastry may have contracted a bit too much during baking), stop pouring and discard the excess custard. Sprinkle the 2 tablespoons of grated Parmesan cheese evenly over the filling, then dot it with the tablespoon of butter, cut into bits.

Baking the Tart

Gently slide the laden shelf into the preheated 325° oven and bake the tart for about 30 minutes, or until the custard is firm and a small table knife inserted into its center emerges almost, but not quite, dry.

Serving the Tart

Remove the tart from the oven and set it on top of a tall coffee can or any similar object, carefully holding the sides of the pan. Check to see if the sides of the pan will slip down easily from the baked shell—if the filling has cooked over, the pastry may stick to the pan at that point. Free any such areas with the point of a small knife, then gently guide the loose rim of the pan down to the table top.

Slide the tart, still on its metal base, onto a serving platter. Serve it at once; or let it cool to lukewarm.

THE PASTRY:
A Fully Baked, Fluted Tart Shell,
    page 57

THE FILLING:
1 package (10 ounces) frozen chopped
    spinach, *defrosted and
    thoroughly drained; or ½ pound
    fresh spinach, cooked
    and thoroughly drained*
2 eggs
¾ cup milk
¼ cup heavy cream
2 coarsely chopped
    hard-cooked eggs (see note to
    Deep-Dish Chicken Pie, page 45)
2 tablespoons finely chopped
    mushrooms; *either dried
    mushrooms—about 12 pieces—
    soaked in warm water for*

*15 minutes, drained, patted dry
with paper towels, and chopped;
or canned mushrooms, drained,
patted dry, and chopped*
2 tablespoons finely
    chopped scallions
1 teaspoon salt
1 teaspoon strained
    fresh lemon juice
⅛ teaspoon ground nutmeg,
    preferably freshly grated
Freshly ground black pepper
2 tablespoons freshly grated
    imported Parmesan cheese
1 tablespoon butter

Preheating the Oven

Slide one of your oven shelves into an upper slot of the oven; set the thermostat at 325° and preheat the oven for 15 minutes.

Making the Filling

A small handful at a time, squeeze the spinach dry; then, using a long sharp knife on a board, chop it as fine as possible.

Break 2 eggs into a 2-quart mixing bowl and, using a fork or a small whisk, beat them for a few seconds,

or only long enough to combine them. Then stir in ¾ cup of milk and ¼ cup of cream. Add the chopped spinach, 2 chopped hard-cooked eggs, 2 tablespoons of chopped mushrooms, 2 tablespoons of chopped scallions, 1 teaspoon of salt, 1 teaspoon of lemon juice, ⅛ teaspoon of nutmeg, and a liberal grinding of black pepper. With the fork or a rubber spatula, stir together thoroughly. Taste for seasoning.

Filling the Tart

Pull the oven shelf forward and place the baked shell on it. Then pour the spinach mixture carefully into the shell. If the filling threatens to overflow (the pastry may have contracted too much when you baked it), stop pouring and discard the excess filling. Sprinkle 2 tablespoons of grated Parmesan cheese over the filling and dot it evenly with the tablespoon of butter, cut into bits.

Baking the Tart

Gently slide the rack back into the preheated 325° oven and bake the tart for about 30 minutes, or until the custard is firm and a table knife inserted into its center emerges almost, but not entirely, dry.

Serving the Tart

Remove the tart from the oven and set it on top of a tall coffee can or any large tall can, carefully holding onto the sides of the pan. Check to see if the sides of the pan will separate easily from the baked shell—if the filling has cooked over at any point, the pastry may adhere to the metal. Free any such areas with the point of a small knife before gently guiding the outer rim of the pan down to the table top.

Slide the spinach tart, still on its metal base, carefully onto a large round serving platter. Serve it at once.

A Savory Tart with Two Cheeses

For some tastes the blue cheese in this tart may be too piquant. If you prefer a milder flavor, substitute for the blue cheese an equal quantity of Camembert or Liederkranz. Cut away the crust after allowing the cheese to soften at room temperature for about half an hour.

A Savory Tart with Two Cheeses   Serves 6

THE PASTRY:
A Fully Baked, Fluted Tart Shell,
   page 57

THE FILLING:
1 package (8 ounces) cream cheese,
   *softened at room temperature
   for 20 to 30 minutes*
1 package (4 ounces) blue cheese,
   *either domestic blue or
   imported bleu, softened
   at room temperature
   for 20 to 30 minutes*

2 tablespoons heavy cream
2 eggs
2 tablespoons finely
   chopped parsley
1 tablespoon grated onion
½ teaspoon salt
1 teaspoon sweet
   Hungarian paprika

Preheating the Oven

Slide one of your oven shelves into an upper slot of the oven; set the thermostat at 325° and preheat the oven for 15 minutes.

Making the Filling

Cream the cream cheese and the blue cheese together by mashing them against the sides of a large, heavy mixing bowl with a large wooden spoon, then beating them vigorously until the mixture is fluffy and smooth.

Beat in 2 tablespoons of cream and, one at a time, break in the 2 eggs, beating sturdily after each addition. When not a trace of the eggs remains, stir in 2 tablespoons of chopped parsley, 1 tablespoon of grated onion, and ½ teaspoon of salt. Taste for seasoning—it may need more salt.

Filling the Tart

Carefully pour the mixture into the tart shell and spread it out evenly with a rubber spatula. Sprinkle the top with the teaspoon of paprika.

Bake the tart in the preheated 325° oven for 30 minutes, or until the filling is firm and a table knife inserted into its center emerges almost, but not entirely, dry.

Serving the Tart

Remove the tart from the oven and set it on top of a tall coffee can or any similar object, carefully holding onto the sides of the pan. Check to see if the sides of the pan will move freely down from the baked shell—if the filling has cooked over at any point, the pastry may be clinging to the metal. Free any such areas with the point of a small knife before guiding the outer rim down to the table top.

Slide the tart, still on its metal base, onto a serving platter. Serve it at once.

Serves 4 to 6

THE PASTRY:
A Partially Baked, Fluted Tart Shell,
   page 64

THE FILLING:
2 cups (about 2 pounds) baking
   potatoes, *peeled, shredded,*
   squeezed, and packed down
2 eggs
¼ cup heavy cream
1 teaspoon salt
Freshly ground black pepper
4 tablespoons butter, *melted*

2 teaspoons caraway seed,
   slightly bruised or crushed
20 inch-thick slices (about 1½
   pounds) of peeled sausage,
   preferably Kielbasa (Polish
   sausage); but if it is
   unavailable, any similar
   garlic-flavored sausage

Preheating the Oven

Slide one of your oven shelves into an upper slot of the oven; set the thermostat at 325° and preheat the oven for 15 minutes.

Making the Filling

Peel the potatoes and drop each into a bowl of cold water as soon as it is finished, to prevent discoloration. When all the potatoes have been peeled, remove them one at a time, pat them dry with paper towels, and shred them directly into a mixing bowl, using the tear-shaped teeth of a stand-up four-sided grater. Work quickly to keep at a minimum the discoloration that appears as shredded potatoes stand. (Discoloration will not affect the taste of the tart, but it will make it less attractive.)

When all the potatoes have been shredded, squeeze them firmly, a handful at a time, to rid them of as much moisture as possible. Drop each handful into a pint-size glass measuring cup as you finish squeezing it, then pack it down. You should have 2 cups of firmly packed shredded potatoes. If you don't, peel, shred, and squeeze another potato with the utmost dispatch.

Break 2 eggs into a 2-quart mixing bowl and, using a fork or a small whisk, beat them for a few seconds, or only long enough to combine them. Stir in ¼ cup of cream, 1 teaspoon of salt, and a liberal grinding of black pepper and continue to stir until the ingredients are well combined. Then add the potatoes and 4 tablespoons of melted butter. Stir mixture well and taste it for seasoning; it may need more salt.

Filling the Tart

Pour the contents of the bowl into the tart shell and spread the potatoes out evenly with a rubber spatula. Sprinkle 2 teaspoons of caraway seed over the filling, then place slightly overlapping slices of sausage around the edge. If the 20 pieces are not enough to make a complete circle, peel and slice more of the sausage.

Baking the Tart

Bake the tart in the preheated 325° oven for 45 minutes. Because some potatoes cook more quickly than others, test the filling for doneness 15 minutes or so before the time is up. The tart is done when the potatoes show no resistance to the point of a small sharp knife.

Serving the Tart

Remove the tart from the oven and set it on a tall coffee can or any similar object. Gently guide the outer rim of the pan down to the table top.

Slide the tart, still on its metal base, onto a serving platter. Serve it at once.

Tomato and Cheese Tart

This is my version, made with Parmesan and Switzerland cheese, of a famous French country tart. The French frequently serve it cold, especially at picnics. I personally prefer it hot; and you can choose between the French and me, or compromise by serving it lukewarm.

Tomato and Cheese Tart

Serves 4

THE PASTRY:
A Fully Baked, Fluted Tart Shell, page 57

THE FILLING:
5 firm but ripe medium-sized tomatoes (about 1½ pounds), *stem ends removed and the tomatoes sliced about ½ inch thick*
1 tablespoon salt
¼ pound Switzerland cheese, *coarsely grated* (about 1 cup, packed down)

Freshly ground black pepper
2 tablespoons finely cut fresh basil *or 1 tablespoon crumbled dried basil*
5 or 6 scallions, *coarsely chopped, including 2 inches of the green part* (about 6 tablespoons)
2 tablespoons freshly grated imported Parmesan cheese
2 tablespoons dry bread crumbs
1 tablespoon butter

A French favorite for picnics, Tomato and Cheese Tart is equally good served hot, lukewarm, or cold.

Preparing the Tomatoes

Sprinkle the tomato slices on both sides with 1 tablespoon of salt, then place the tomatoes on a wire cake rack set over paper towels or a large shallow pan. Let them drain for 30 minutes. Then spread the tomatoes on a double layer of paper towels and gently pat them dry with more towels.

Preheating the Oven

Slide one of your oven shelves into an upper slot of the oven; set the thermostat at 325° and preheat the oven for 15 minutes.

Filling the Tart

Spread the cup of grated Switzerland cheese evenly in the tart shell. Arrange the sliced tomatoes in overlapping concentric circles so that they cover the cheese completely. Season the tomatoes evenly with a liberal grinding of black pepper, and scatter 2 tablespoons of fresh basil (or 1 tablespoon of dried basil) and 6 tablespoons of chopped scallions over the top.

In a small bowl, combine 2 tablespoons of grated Parmesan cheese with 2 tablespoons of bread crumbs, stirring the mixture with a fork or your fingers. Sprinkle the crumbs evenly over the filling and dot the top with the tablespoon of butter, cut into bits.

Baking the Tart

Bake the tart in the preheated 325° oven for 30 minutes, or just until the tomatoes are still slightly resistant when pressed with your fingers and the crumb-cheese topping is lightly browned.

Serving the Tart

Remove the tart from the oven and place it on top of a tall coffee can or any can of similar size, carefully holding onto the sides of the pan.

Check to see if the sides will come away easily from the baked shell—if the filling has cooked over at any point, the pastry may stick to the metal. Free any such areas with the point of a small knife before guiding the outer rim down to the table top.

Slide the tart, still on its metal base, onto a round serving platter. Let the tart rest for about 5 minutes, then serve it.

Fruit-topped Custard Tart with Apricot or Currant Glaze

Although I have suggested fresh strawberries for this incomparable fruit tart with a custard base, you may, if you prefer, use any other fruit of your choice. You might consider, among others, fresh berries of any kind; or canned, drained fruit halves—peaches, pears, or apricots. Frozen fruits, thoroughly defrosted and drained, make a most effective topping, too. Whatever the fruit you *use, arrange it as attractively as you can on the custard base.*

The glaze, too, may be changed. Simply substitute an equal amount of currant jelly for the apricot jam. It is unnecessary to rub the jelly through a strainer; just dissolve it in 2 tablespoons of water and simmer the mixture for a few minutes until it thickens. Cool it to lukewarm before glazing the tart.

Fruit-topped Custard Tart with Apricot or Currant Glaze   Serves 6

THE PASTRY:
A Fully Baked, Fluted Tart Shell
   (page 57), *still in its pan*

- -

THE FILLING:

2 eggs	1 teaspoon vanilla
3 tablespoons sugar	1 cup milk
2 tablespoons flour	¾ cup chilled heavy cream
Pinch of salt	1 to 1½ quarts fresh,
1 envelope plain (unflavored) gelatin	ripe strawberries

- -

THE GLAZE:
1 cup apricot jam
2 tablespoons water

Preparing the Tart for Filling

Set the tart shell, still in its pan, on top of a tall coffee can or any object of similar size, and let the sides of the pan drop down. With a wide metal spatula, lift the pastry shell off its base and slide it onto a round serving platter. (Handle the shell gently, or you may break off bits of the sides. If such an unfortunate event should occur, see repair instructions on page 64.) Set the shell aside while you prepare the filling.

Preparing the Filling

With a rotary beater, beat 2 eggs in a medium-sized mixing bowl for a few seconds, or just long enough to combine them. Then add 3 tablespoons of sugar and continue to beat the eggs until the mixture is thick enough to fall in a sluggish ribbon when the beater is lifted out of the bowl. Add 2 tablespoons of flour, a pinch of salt, the gelatin, and the teaspoon of vanilla. Beat once more until the added ingredients are thoroughly absorbed.

1. After custard filling is poured into baked tart shell, it is chilled until it is not quite completely firm.

In a heavy 2-quart saucepan heat 1 cup of milk over moderate heat until small bubbles form around the edges.

To make the custard, slowly pour the hot milk into the egg mixture, stirring it continuously with a wooden spoon. Now return the mixture to the saucepan, running a rubber spatula around the bowl to make certain you have left none of it behind, and set the pan over low heat.

Cook the custard slowly without ever letting it come to a boil, stirring it constantly with the spatula and making sure you occasionally run the spatula around the sides of the pan and especially the crease, where the custard tends to coagulate. When the custard has thickened fairly heavily and is smooth, scrape it back into the mixing bowl and refrigerate it, uncovered, for about 15 minutes, or until it has thickened further and cooled completely.

Then, with a rotary beater, whip ¾ cup of chilled heavy cream in a chilled, medium-sized bowl until the cream forms firm but still slightly wavering peaks on the beater when you lift it up.

With a rubber spatula, immediately scrape the whipped cream over the custard. Slowly fold the two together, cutting down and bringing the heavier mass up over the lighter one just until no streaks of cream show. If at any point the mixture threatens to become lumpy—as sometimes happens—beat it slowly with the rotary beater until it is smooth. Then pour the custard into the waiting tart shell and smooth it out with the spatula.

Refrigerate the tart once more until the custard has become not quite completely firm—it should jiggle when you shake the pan gently.

Meanwhile, hull the strawberries and, one at a time, dip them quickly into cold water. Pat them gently but thoroughly dry with paper towels, then arrange them in concentric rings on the custard, starting around the sides and placing them stem ends down. If you don't have enough ber-

2. Starting around outside, strawberries are set in rings on the filling, close together and stem ends down.

3. Warm apricot glaze is spooned carefully over berries. Tart is then refrigerated so that glaze may set.

ries to cover the custard completely, space them farther apart.

Return the tart to the refrigerator while you make the glaze.

Making the Glaze

Place the cupful of apricot jam in a sieve set over a small saucepan. Rub the jam through the sieve with the back of a spoon and discard any pulp left in the sieve. Stir 2 tablespoons of water into the apricot purée, then, stirring it constantly with a spoon, simmer the mixture for about 5 minutes, or until it thickens to a syrup-like consistency.

Remove the pan from the heat and let the glaze cool only to lukewarm. If you let it cool too much, it will be too thick to pour, but don't be concerned if this happens—merely reheat it and let it cool to the proper temperature.

Glazing the Tart

Remove the tart from the refrigerator and dribble a light coating of the glaze over each strawberry, letting the excess cover any exposed custard. Refrigerate the tart again for at least an hour, or until the glaze sets and the custard is firm.

Serving the Tart

The finished tart can safely remain in the refrigerator for 6 to 8 hours. But if it has chilled that long, it might not be a bad idea to allow the tart to rest at room temperature for about 15 minutes before you serve it.

Tartlets

Tartlets differ from tarts, as their name implies, mainly in the matter of size—they are small tarts. Although French tart pastry may be used to line the tartlet pans, I have included a recipe for an alternative (and richer) pastry dough in which an egg takes the place of water. Do not make the mistake, however, of using tartlet pastry for tarts; it is difficult to handle when lining a large pan.

Three hours, or even a day, before you want to use this pastry, make it and refrigerate it, well wrapped in foil or plastic.

Chilling the ingredients is not the crucial element it is in making the French tart pastry. But it is indeed essential that you chill this dough thoroughly after you have made it. Because this pastry is so short—or, in other words, because it contains a large amount of butter in proportion to the flour, to say nothing of the egg—you will find it virtually impossible to roll out unless it has been chilled to considerable firmness beforehand.

As for my tartlet fillings, they are similar to those for the tarts, but they are in general more custardy in texture and more piquant in flavor, as befits morsels you will probably serve as accompaniments for drinks.

Cheese Tartlets

Makes 24

THE PASTRY:

1½ cups sifted all-purpose flour
½ teaspoon salt
8 tablespoons butter
 (a quarter-pound stick),
 cut into ¼-inch slices
 and thoroughly chilled
1 egg, slightly beaten
2 tablespoons unsifted flour

THE FILLING:

2 eggs
1 cup heavy cream
¼ teaspoon salt
⅛ teaspoon freshly ground
 black pepper
⅛ teaspoon nutmeg,
 preferably freshly grated
¼ teaspoon dry mustard
½ cup grated Switzerland cheese,
 packed down

Mixing and Chilling the Dough

Sift 1½ cups of flour with ½ teaspoon of salt into a large mixing bowl and add the slices of chilled butter. Toss the butter pieces to coat them with the flour. Then, using a pastry blender, cut into the butter with small, quick chopping motions to distribute it evenly through the flour.

When the mixture is as uniform as corn meal, pour over it the lightly beaten egg. Now substitute two table knives for the pastry blender and, using a criss-cross motion, cut and stir the egg thoroughly into the dough, scraping the knives across each other from time to time to remove the pastry sticking to them.

Gather the dough together in your hands and mold it into a ball. Press the ball against any stray pellets of dough in the bowl and work them in.

Now hold the dough over the bowl and sprinkle the 2 tablespoons of unsifted flour over it, rotating the ball until a film of flour covers the dough lightly and uniformly.

Wrap the dough in plastic wrap, or enclose it in a plastic bag, and refrigerate it for at least 3 hours, or for as long as two days.

Rolling the Dough

Remove the dough from the refrigerator and let it soften slightly, just until you can press a finger into it fairly easily. Pat it out on a floured pastry cloth to a circle about 4 inches across, then roll it out into a circle a little less than ⅛ inch thick, using the technique described in the recipe for a tart shell (page 57).

With a 3-inch cookie or biscuit cutter, cut out rounds and lay them on a long strip of wax paper.

Quickly gather together the pastry scraps and knead them into a ball, using a little extra flour if the scraps are too soft. Roll them into another circle of the same thickness as the first. Cut out rounds as before. You should have 24 pastry rounds when all the dough has been rolled and cut. (It may reassure you to know that rolling and rerolling this particular dough will not affect its tex-

Tips and Techniques ...
Freezing and keeping
tart and tartlet pastry

I don't recommend freezing a fully baked, filled tart of any kind, because the moisture generated during the defrosting process will turn the tart sodden.

Unfilled tart and tartlet shells, either unbaked or baked, may be frozen, provided they are securely wrapped in heavy-duty foil.

An unbaked frozen tart shell may be baked without defrosting it first. A frozen, baked tart shell should not be defrosted; fill it quickly and bake it immediately in its frozen state. In either case the baking time will be the same as for an unfrozen shell. Tart pastry may be frozen for up to two months if it is well wrapped and kept at a temperature below 0°.

If you want to store pastry for only a day or two, line the tart pan with pastry, cover it with plastic wrap, and refrigerate it. Fill and bake the shell immediately after removing it from the refrigerator.

ture to any appreciable degree. In this respect, it is quite different from my American pie crust.)

Lining the Muffin Tins

Line each muffin cup with a pastry round in the following fashion: Lay the round over the cup. Then lift up the sides of the round with the fingers of both hands and gently encourage the pastry to fall into place, exerting slight downward pressure. Now run your fingertip around the bottom crease of the cup to mold the pastry gently against the sides. The sides will fold into small pleats which will give them a somewhat irregular appearance. Don't fuss with this now; your primary concern should be to make sure that the pastry reaches the top of each muffin cup, or even rises above the rim.

Refrigerating the Pastry

Refrigerate the pastry-lined muffin tins for at least half an hour while you prepare the filling. Chilling the pastry will firm it so that you can shape and mold the cups more symmetrically if you wish to improve their appearance.

Preheating the Oven

Slide one of your oven shelves into a slot in the lower third of the oven; set the thermostat at 450° and preheat the oven for 15 minutes while you make the filling.

Making the Filling

Break 2 eggs into a 2-quart mixing bowl and, using a fork or a small whisk, beat them for a moment, or only long enough to combine them. Then add the cup of heavy cream, ¼ teaspoon of salt, ⅛ teaspoon of freshly ground black pepper, ⅛ teaspoon of nutmeg, and ¼ teaspoon of dry mustard and stir until the ingredients are thoroughly mixed. Taste for seasoning; the mixture may need more salt and pepper.

Filling the Tartlets

Now remove the lined muffin tins from the refrigerator and put an equal amount (about a teaspoonful) of the grated Switzerland cheese into each of the 24 tartlets.

Pour 1 tablespoon of the custard mixture into each tartlet. As the tartlets rest, the cheese will absorb some of the custard and you can go around a second time, adding any remaining custard until the tartlets are filled almost to the brim. Make certain that the filling doesn't overflow.

Baking the Tartlets

Carefully transfer the filled tartlet pans to the preheated 450° oven and bake them undisturbed for 10 minutes. Then lower the heat to 325° and bake them 5 to 8 minutes longer, or until the filling has puffed and the pastry edges have become golden brown.

Serving the Tartlets

Run a table knife around the sides of each tartlet, then carefully remove them from their cups. Arrange them on a large platter and serve them at once. The filling will sink a bit as the tartlets cool, but this is as it should be.

Crabmeat Tartlets

Makes 24

THE PASTRY:
2 muffin tins lined with
  tartlet pastry (see preceding
  recipe for Cheese Tartlets)

THE FILLING:
2 eggs
1 cup heavy cream
1/2 teaspoon salt
1/8 teaspoon white pepper
1/2 cup fresh crabmeat, *packed down; or* canned crabmeat (about half of a 6 1/2 -ounce can), *thoroughly drained and picked over for bits of shell or cartilage; or 1/2 cup frozen crabmeat, defrosted and drained*
2 tablespoons freshly grated imported Parmesan cheese

Refrigerating the Pastry

Set the pastry-lined muffin tins in the refrigerator for at least half an hour.

Preheating the Oven

Slide one of your oven shelves into a slot in the lower third of the oven; set the thermostat at 450° and preheat the oven for 15 minutes.

Making the Filling

Break 2 eggs into a 2-quart mixing bowl and, using a fork or a small whisk, beat them a few seconds, or only long enough to combine them. Then stir in the cup of heavy cream, ½ teaspoon of salt, and ⅛ teaspoon of white pepper. Stir gently until the ingredients are well combined. Taste the custard mixture for seasoning; it

may need more salt and pepper.

Now remove the lined muffin tins from the refrigerator and put about a teaspoonful of the crabmeat into each of the 24 tartlets. If it doesn't work out to absolute mathematical perfection, steal a little from some tartlets so that all the cups have about the same amount.

Pour 1 tablespoon of the custard mixture into each tartlet. As they rest the crabmeat will absorb the custard and you can go around a second time, adding any remaining custard until the tartlets are filled almost to the brim. Make certain that the filling doesn't overflow. Now sprinkle a little of the freshly grated Parmesan cheese over the top of each tartlet.

Baking the Tartlets

Carefully transfer the filled pans to the preheated 450° oven and bake them undisturbed for 10 minutes. Then lower the heat to 325° and bake them for 5 to 8 minutes longer, or until the filling has puffed and the pastry edges are golden brown.

Serving the Tartlets

Run a table knife around the sides of each tartlet, then carefully remove the tartlets from their cups. Arrange them on a large platter and serve them at once. The filling will sink a bit as it cools, but this is as it should be.

Bread Tartlet Shells

Because of their simplicity, don't underestimate the extraordinary effect these tiny toasted bread shells create. They take only minutes to make and can be filled with Curried Tuna Pâté, page 97, or Herbed Cream Cheese, page 98, or any of the variations suggested in those recipes.

Fill the bread tartlet shells while they are still warm, mounding the filling as generously as you like. You need not be limited to the fillings suggested above—you can use any other filling your imagination dictates. For a more robust tartlet, you might even consider so unorthodox a filling as hot baked beans, generously spiked with any seasoning of your choice.

Because the bread cases are so porous, I must caution you, however, about the type of filling that can be actually baked in the tartlets. You can fill them before baking with any fairly dense cooked filling, but not with a custardy or moist mixture that would seep through the cases during baking.

Whatever filling you choose, these charming constructions make wonderful accompaniments to drinks of any kind.

Bread Tartlet Shells

Makes 24

For making the shells, you will
    need 24 slices of fresh
    homemade-type
    packaged white bread

Preheating the Oven

Slide one of your oven shelves into the center slot of the oven, set the thermostat at 375°, and preheat the oven for 15 minutes.

Making and Baking the Shells

Stamp out the center of each slice of bread with a 3-inch cookie cutter. Fill each muffin cup with a round of bread in the following fashion: Lay a circle of bread over the muffin cup and, lifting the circle slightly, gently mold it into the cup with your fingers. Then press your forefinger around the bottom crease so that the bread takes on the shape of the cup. Don't fuss with this too much, lest you tear the fragile bread.

Bake the bread tartlet shells in the preheated 375° oven for 10 to 15 minutes, or only until they are light golden brown. They burn easily, so keep your eye on them. When the shells have reached the color you desire and have become fairly firm, remove the muffin tins from the oven and carefully lift each shell out of its cup.

The tartlet shells may be filled at once and served immediately. Or you may refrigerate the filled shells, but let them return to room temperature before serving.

Freezing the Shells

You may find it advantageous to know that the unfilled tartlet shells may be wrapped in aluminum foil or enclosed in a plastic bag and frozen. Don't defrost them before using; simply preheat your oven to 325°, place the shells on a cookie sheet, and heat them for about 10 minutes, or until they are thoroughly defrosted and crisp.

Chou paste is the versatile basis for a savory cheese ring; for small, filled canapé puffs; and for the almond-topped, cream-filled dessert ring called Paris-Brest.

Cream Puffs and Savory Puffs

Whether the French or the Italians invented these extraordinary puffs is a moot point, but the French name, *pâte à choux,* is generally used for the dough. This can be translated loosely as "paste in the form of cabbages." Presumably this name derives from the fact that the small or large puffs made from it look, to some French eyes, like cabbages—they certainly don't to mine. But the name is here to stay and we may as well use it, but in its shortened Anglo-French version—*chou* paste.

Chou paste is the easiest of pastries to prepare. It consists of water, butter, flour, and eggs: the butter is melted in the boiling water, the flour is stirred into it to make a paste, and then the eggs are beaten in. This simple preparation, however, has the most magical properties. When baked in the oven it explodes into the most remarkable shapes imaginable.

Chou paste puffs up for entirely different reasons than, for example, a soufflé does. Basically it is the *air* beaten into the egg whites that are folded into the soufflé base which rises when it is subjected to oven heat. The *pâte à choux* rises in another fashion and for another reason. The eggs are partially cooked during their beating into the hot paste. Then, when this rather sturdy paste is heated rapidly in baking, the steam in the mixture doesn't just cause it to expand—it literally causes an explosion and gives the puffs their fanciful shapes.

I therefore stress the need for speed of preparation, whether you make the paste by hand or in an electric mixer, because the paste must remain hot (but off the heat) while the eggs are beaten into it if they are to undergo this partial cooking. If you add the eggs too slowly and beat the paste too long after each addition, by the time the last egg is added the paste will be too cool. This crucial element of speed makes the difference between glorious success and partial or complete failure.

Utensils You Will Need for Chou Puffs...

Pastry Bags   These are available in sizes from 10 to 24 inches. You should own at least three, ranging from small to large. If you can't acquire all of them, then settle for a 16-inch one. The bags may be made of either nylon or canvas. Each has its advantages. Nylon is easy to clean and does not retain odors. For whipped cream, a canvas bag is preferable; unlike the smooth and slippery nylon, canvas takes a firm hold on the whipped cream and gives you more control as you pipe it out.

Pastry Tips   The sizes and patterns of pastry tips are designated by name and number. If you can, by all means buy a complete set of decorative and plain tips. If you must limit your purchase, settle for Star Tip No. 9 and Plain Tips Nos. 3, 6, and 9.

Plus — The same mixing bowls, cookie sheets, cake racks, wooden spoons, and heavy 2-quart saucepan that you need for making pies and tarts.

And a Few of Your Basic Kitchen Utensils:

An electric blender
Measuring spoons
Pastry brushes
Two sets of measuring cups
   (one set for dry ingredients,
   one set for liquids)
Wooden spoons
Whisks
Rotary beater
Rubber spatulas

Not Necessary, But Helpful to Have

Electric Mixer   A model with a pastry arm or paddle.

Makes about 2 cups*

1 cup water
6 tablespoons butter
1¼ cups sifted all-purpose flour
½ teaspoon salt

1 cup of eggs (4 whole eggs plus, possibly, one additional white, or part of an additional white, to make precisely one cupful), *beaten with a whisk only long enough to combine the yolks and whites*

Hand Method

In a heavy 2-quart saucepan, combine 1 cup of water, 6 tablespoons of butter, cut into pieces, and ½ teaspoon of salt. Set over high heat and cook, stirring constantly, until the butter has dissolved and the water has begun to boil all over its surface.

Remove the pan from the heat instantly—if you let the mixture continue to boil, part of the water will evaporate and you will end up with less liquid than you need. Dump in the flour in one fell swoop and stir the ingredients together vigorously with a large wooden spoon. After a few seconds of hard stirring—all around the pan, including the sides —the mixture will have the appearance of somewhat leaden but smooth mashed potatoes.

Return the pan to moderate heat

and continue to stir briskly for 4 or 5 seconds—no more—until you can hold the whole mass up in your spoon and the pan is almost as clean as it was when you started.

Speed of mixing is now the crucial factor. With your spoon, make a deep hollow in the center of the paste (but it should not be so deep as to expose the bottom of the pan).

Tips and Techniques...
Flavorings and sweetenings
Like pie pastries—and tart pastry, too, for that matter— plain chou *pastry is meant to be, almost always, a* texture enclosing a taste. *Therefore sweetening it (or adding flavoring, when you use the paste in making desserts) is unnecessary. However, when the paste is used in certain recipes, such as that for the* gougère, *other ingredients are essential, as you will see.*

*Changing the quantity: Do not attempt to double or halve this recipe, or the results may be unpredictable. If you need more than the 2 cups of paste my recipe yields, make two separate batches. If you need half the amount, make the full amount and wrap the surplus in foil and refrigerate it for another use.

Using a dry-measuring cup, immediately scoop up about a quarter-cup of the lightly beaten eggs and pour it into the hollow. Briskly stir the paste into the eggs and continue to stir for a few seconds, until the slippery strands come together again and become a comparatively firm mass.

Without waiting a second, form another hollow and pour in another quarter-cup of eggs and combine as before. Add the third and fourth quarter-cups of eggs quickly, beating each addition in the same fashion.

After the last addition, beat the mixture vigorously for another moment—and the *chou* paste is done.

Let it cool to lukewarm or room temperature before using it in any of the recipes that follow.

Electric Mixer Method

If you have an electric mixer equipped with a paddle or a pastry

Tips and Techniques...
A note on butter
I prefer sweet (unsalted) butter for making chou *paste as well as for other pastries. If you use salt butter, reduce the amount of salt called for by one half.*

Tips and Techniques...
Mixing methods
By far the most effective method of preparing chou *paste is to beat it by hand. This makes it possible to judge the state of the paste at every stage. An electric mixer with a pastry arm may be used if you wish.*

arm, you can make the paste with less physical exertion.

Follow the directions for cooking the basic mixture of water, butter, and flour; then, after heating it for the 4 or 5 seconds required, immediately transfer it to the mixer bowl. (To insure predictability of the result, you might, before cooking the paste, fill the mixer bowl with very hot water. At the time of transfer, empty the bowl and dry it before adding the hot paste.)

Proceed as for the hand-beaten paste, adding the eggs a quarter-cup at a time and running the machine at low speed (to prevent splattering) during each addition until the eggs are partially absorbed, then beating at high speed just until the separated strands of dough have come together. Continue adding the eggs in quarter-cup amounts, lowering, then raising, the speed after each addition. Complete the operation as quickly as possible.

90

After all the eggs have been absorbed, you may beat the mixture 4 or 5 seconds longer for good measure, but don't overdo it. Overbeating will not ruin the paste, but neither will it improve it.

Storing the Paste

If you want to store the paste, cool it and transfer it to a bowl, cover it closely with plastic wrap, and refrigerate it for as long as a day or two.

Be sure to remove it from the refrigerator at least 2 hours before you want to use it, because it must be at room temperature if it is to behave as it should when it is baked. (I must warn you not to attempt to hasten the warming-up process by heating chilled paste on the stove. Even a few seconds' cooking at this point will ruin it.)

Tips and Techniques . . .
Making paste or puffs
ahead of time

Chou *paste may be made hours before you plan to use it, although it is at its best when used immediately, even while still warm.*

If you make the paste ahead of time, cover it with plastic wrap lest a hard crust form on the surface. (This would prevent the paste from rising to maximum volume.)

If you will be using the paste within about 2 or 3 hours, leave it, covered, at room temperature. If you have refrigerated it for a day or so, let it come to room temperature before using it.

Tips and Techniques . . .
One factor relating to flour

The ability of your flour to absorb moisture can affect your results with chou *paste to a certain extent. If the flour you use happens to be resistant to moisture, your puffs may spread a bit instead of rising loftily. In that case, I'd advise trying another brand or two of flour, following the recipe precisely, until your results are perfect. I would not recommend increasing the amount of flour or reducing the amount of egg unless you are more expert than most home bakers.*

As I noted earlier, all my puff recipes have been tested with Gold Medal flour.

Cream-filled puffs with a hot chocolate sauce are always listed on French menus as profiteroles au chocolat, *but by any name this is an elegant dessert. The origin of the word* profiteroles *is almost impossible to pinpoint precisely, but I do know it was in common use in the sixteenth century and means, literally, "small profit." Why this term was used by the bakers who first made* profiteroles *is a mystery to culinary historians, because the puffs require few ingredients, not one of them rare or exotic. The chocolate, then a great rarity, was a later addition.*

Cream-filled Puffs with Hot Cocoa Sauce

Makes about 35 cream puffs
about 1½ inches in diameter;
serves 6 to 8

THE CREAM PUFFS:
1 recipe *Chou* Paste, page 89

FOR PREPARING THE PANS:
1 tablespoon butter,
    softened at room temperature
4 tablespoons unsifted flour

THE GLAZE:
1 egg white
2 teaspoons water

THE FILLING:
1 cup chilled heavy cream
2 tablespoons sugar
1 teaspoon vanilla

THE TOPPING:
Confectioners' sugar

THE HOT COCOA SAUCE:
1½ cups sugar
1 cup water
1½ cups unsweetened cocoa

*Tips and Techniques . . .
Only one pan*
The only pans you will use for baking pâte à choux *preparations will be baking sheets. Because the paste must expand into free and fanciful forms, it is never enclosed in a pan with sides or in a mold.*

Preheating the Oven

Slide one of your oven shelves into the top slot of the oven and another into the lowest slot; then set the thermostat at 450° and preheat the oven for 15 minutes.

Preparing the Pans

Using a pastry brush, the tablespoon of softened butter, and the 4 tablespoons of unsifted flour, grease

*Among the most elegant of desserts,
tiny chocolate-sauced cream puffs are surprisingly simple to make.*

and flour 2 cookie sheets. Invert each sheet and rap it on a table to knock off the excess flour.

Shaping the Puffs

Drop heaping teaspoonfuls of the *chou* paste onto the cookie sheet, leaving about 2 inches between mounds. (You can use a pastry bag and a No. 6 plain tip for shaping the puffs, if you wish.) Do not crowd the puffs—they need space to double in size as they bake.

If you have dropped the puffs from a spoon, shape each mound with the back of a teaspoon so that they are higher than they are wide. (Don't fuss with this too much. The charm of these puffs is the variety of forms into which they explode.)

Bake the puffs undisturbed for 5 minutes; then lower the heat to 425° and bake them for 10 to 15 minutes longer, or until they have puffed to about twice their original size, feel firm to the touch, and have turned golden brown. To make sure they are thoroughly baked, break one puff open. If the inside is doughy, quickly close the oven door and bake the puffs a few minutes longer.

Turn off the oven, and, one pan at a time, remove the puffs. Pierce them (still on their sheets) in the side with the point of a small sharp knife. This will allow the steam to escape and

Glazing the Puffs

In a small mixing bowl, beat the egg white and 2 teaspoons of water with a whisk only long enough to combine them.

Dip a pastry brush into the mixture and brush each puff lightly; but don't allow any of the wash (as it is called) to drip down onto the baking sheet. (This could discourage the puffs from rising as high as they should.)

Baking the Puffs

Set one cookie sheet on the upper shelf of the preheated 450° oven and the other sheet on the lower shelf.

To shape puffs with a pastry bag: First step is to turn top of bag back. Then drop the metal tip into position. Center, a rubber spatula is the best utensil for filling the bag.

Dough is scraped off as spatula is withdrawn. Right, the gathered top is held in one hand while bag is squeezed with other hand. This forces out puffs.

prevent the puffs from becoming soggy. Then return the puffs to the turned-off oven and let them dry, with the oven door closed, for 5 minutes.

Transfer the puffs to wire cake racks and cool them thoroughly.

Making the Filling

In a chilled 2-quart bowl beat 1 cup of chilled heavy cream with a rotary beater for a minute or two, or just until it has thickened lightly. Then add 2 tablespoons of sugar and 1 teaspoon of vanilla and continue beating until the cream forms firm but still slightly wavering peaks on the beater when it is lifted and held upright over the bowl.

Filling and Serving the Puffs

Carefully cut each cream puff in half horizontally and use a small spoon to scrape out any moist paste inside. Drop a heaping teaspoonful or more of the whipped cream into the lower half of each shell, then gently replace the top. Arrange the puffs on a large serving platter.

Ideally, they should be served at once. Refrigerate them if you must, but for no longer than 10 or 15 minutes or so, or the cream will turn the puffs soggy.

Just before serving, dust each puff lightly with powdered sugar, using

To shape puffs with spoons: Drop heaping teaspoonfuls of dough onto pan, using a second spoon as a pusher.

a perforated shaker if you have one, or a small flour sifter or sieve.

Serve with a bowl of Hot Cocoa Sauce.

Making the Hot Cocoa Sauce

In a 2-quart saucepan, stir 1½ cups of sugar with 1 cup of water only long enough to combine them. Then cook the mixture over moderate heat until it comes to a rolling boil and boil it briskly and undisturbed for 2 minutes.

Remove the syrup from the heat and, beating it rapidly with a whisk, add 1½ cups of cocoa and continue to beat until the sauce is smooth and thick and has a satiny look.

If the sauce is too thick for your taste, thin it with a little water or, if you like, with heavy cream. If the sauce does not seem sweet enough, add sugar to taste, stirring the sauce constantly over moderate heat until the sugar dissolves.

You may make this sauce successfully ahead of time and reheat it just before serving.

Tips and Techniques...
Freezing the paste or puffs

I do not recommend freezing chou *paste in its uncooked state. When defrosted and baked it will indeed rise again, but to only half the level of unfrozen paste.*

You may, however, freeze baked, unfilled chou *puffs, provided they are wrapped securely in plastic wrap and then in foil. Before using the frozen puffs, bake them briefly, without defrosting, on a cake rack in a preheated 325° oven. Bake just until crisp.*

Unfilled baked puffs that have been thoroughly cooled may be stored for up to 3 days in an airtight container. Before using them, heat them on a rack in a preheated 350° oven for 2 or 3 minutes, and then cool them on the rack until they are crisp.

Small Puffs Filled with Curried Tuna Pâté

If you prefer another pâté *mixture to the tuna, you may substitute one of the following: Drained canned salmon; frozen cooked lobster, defrosted and well drained; drained, canned minced clams; or cooked shrimp.*

However—and this is important— do not use any of the liquid drained from any of these fish. Instead, increase the amount of vegetable oil by about 1 tablespoon when you purée *the fish.*

Seasonings for any of these pâtés

may be changed at will. For example, omit the curry powder and use liberal amounts of freshly ground pepper instead. Or stir into the mixture a tablespoon or more of any finely chopped or finely cut fresh herb you may have on hand.

Any left-over pâté may be spread on toast or crackers to make canapés.

Small Puffs Filled with Curried Tuna Pâté

Makes 35 puffs

THE PUFFS:
35 small *chou* puffs, *baked and cooled as directed in the recipe for* Cream-filled Puffs with Hot Cocoa Sauce, page 92

THE FILLING:
1 can (7 ounces) tuna fish packed in oil, *coarsely shredded, with its juices*

½ cup coarsely chopped onions (about 1 medium onion)

2 teaspoons strained fresh lemon juice

4 tablespoons vegetable oil

8 tablespoons butter (a quarter-pound stick), *softened at room temperature*

½ teaspoon salt

2 teaspoons curry powder

Making the Pâté

Empty the tuna fish and all its juices into the jar of an electric blender. Add ½ cup of chopped onions, 2 teaspoons of lemon juice, and 3 tablespoons of the vegetable oil, reserving 1 tablespoon. Cover and blend at high speed for about a minute. Then turn off the blender, scrape down the sides of the jar with a rubber spatula, re-cover it and re-sume blending at high speed for a few seconds, or until the purée is smooth. (If at any point the blender clogs, stop the machine and add the remaining tablespoon of vegetable oil, then resume the blending.) Set the purée aside.

In a medium-sized mixing bowl cream 8 tablespoons of butter. Beat in ½ teaspoon of salt and 2 teaspoons of curry powder. Then, tablespoon by tablespoon, beat in the tuna-fish purée and continue to beat until the mixture is smooth. Taste for seasoning and add more salt and lemon juice if you think it needs it.

The *pâté* will be quite fluid at this point, but don't be concerned. Simply cover the bowl with plastic wrap and refrigerate the mixture for about 2 hours, or until it is about the consistency of cream cheese.

Filling and Serving the Puffs

Cut the *chou* puffs in half horizontally, and with a small spoon scrape out any moist paste inside. Fill the bottom of each shell with a teaspoon or more of the *pâté* and set the upper halves in place, allowing a little filling to show.

These puffs are best if they are served at once. If they must wait, you may cover them with plastic wrap and refrigerate them for up to 6 hours. Before serving them, remove the puffs from the refrigerator and let them rest at room temperature for about 10 minutes. This will allow the *pâté* to soften a bit to the velvety consistency it should have.

Small Puffs Filled with Herbed Cream Cheese

In the filling for these puffs you may, of course, use any other fresh herb of your choice in place of the chives. Or, if you wish, substitute finely chopped scallions for the chives. The filling, like the tuna pâté *in the preceding recipe, may be spread on toast or crackers or heaped in bread tartlet shells, page 84, to make canapés.*

Small Puffs Filled with Herbed Cream Cheese *Makes 35 puffs*

THE PUFFS:
35 small *chou* puffs, *baked and cooled* (see the recipe for Cream-filled Puffs with Hot Cocoa Sauce, page 92)

THE FILLING:
1 package (8 ounces) cream cheese, *softened at room temperature*
2 tablespoons butter, *softened at room temperature*
2 tablespoons heavy cream

½ teaspoon salt
Freshly ground black pepper
1 tablespoon finely cut chives, or 2 tablespoons frozen chopped chives

Making the Filling

In a medium-sized mixing bowl, cream the softened cream cheese and 2 tablespoons of softened butter together until the mixture is smooth and fluffy. Beat in 2 tablespoons of cream a tablespoon at a time, then stir in ½ teaspoon of salt, a liberal grinding of black pepper, and 1 tablespoon of finely cut fresh chives or 2 tablespoons of frozen chopped chives. Taste for seasoning; the mixture may need more salt or more chives.

Cover the bowl with plastic wrap and refrigerate the mixture for about an hour, or until it is moderately firm.

Filling and Serving the Puffs

Cut the *chou* puffs in half horizontally and with a small spoon scrape out any moist paste inside.

Tips and Techniques...
When to fill the puffs

For the most part, refrigeration is the natural enemy of filled chou *puffs; therefore I don't recommend this restaurant practice — the moisture in the refrigerator and that in the filling will, between them, give the puffs the texture of damp cardboard.*

Try to serve puffs at once, if they are meant to be served hot, or they will become soggy. Or if they are to be served cold, filled with whipped cream, ice cream, or another dessert filling, fill them just before serving.

Cream fillings should never—and this should be emphasized—should never be allowed to sit at room temperature for more than a few minutes, for two reasons. The cream tastes best when properly chilled; and warmth may produce souring or, even worse, permit bacteria to multiply to an actually dangerous level.

Fill the bottom of each shell with a teaspoonful or more of the filling and set the upper halves in place.

These are best when served at once. If the puffs must wait, you may cover them and refrigerate them for up to 6 hours. Before serving them, remove the puffs from the refrigerator and let them rest at room temperature for about 10 minutes. This will allow the cheese filling to soften to a velvety consistency.

Savory Puffed Cheese Ring

This puffed cheese ring, called a gougère by the French, originated in Burgundy in the thirteenth century. It was then, and still is, torn into pieces and served with a glass of good Burgundy wine. We in America need not be so traditional. The ring makes a perfect accompaniment to drinks of any kind and may even be served in place of bread, with a salad. Not the least of its charms is that it can be served either hot or warm; and some people even prefer it at room temperature.

Savory Puffed Cheese Ring

Makes two 9-inch rings

THE PASTRY:

1 recipe *Chou* Paste, page 89
1 teaspoon prepared mustard
1 teaspoon salt
1¼ cups coarsely grated imported
    Switzerland cheese;
    or freshly grated imported
    Parmesan cheese; or a
    combination of the two
    in any proportions you like

FOR PREPARING THE PANS:

1 tablespoon butter,
    softened at room temperature
4 tablespoons unsifted flour

THE GLAZE:

1 egg
2 teaspoons water

Preheating the Oven

Slide one of your oven shelves into the topmost slot of the oven and slide another into the lowest slot; then set the thermostat at 450° and preheat the oven for 15 minutes.

Making the Pastry

Place the *chou* paste in a large mixing bowl and add 1 teaspoon of prepared mustard and 1 teaspoon of salt. Using a wooden spoon, beat the paste very vigorously for a moment,

then beat in 1 cup of the grated cheese, reserving ¼ cup.

Preparing the Pans

Using a pastry brush, the tablespoon of softened butter, and the 4 tablespoons of unsifted flour, grease and flour 2 cookie sheets. Invert each sheet and rap it on a table to knock off the excess flour.

Using a 7-inch round cake pan or any pan or lid of the same diameter as a guide, press the outline of a circle on the floured surface of each sheet.

Shaping the Rings

Place heaping tablespoonfuls of the *chou* paste side by side around each circle to form 2 rings. (Or, if you wish, pipe the paste into 2 rings, using a pastry bag and a plain No. 9 tip.)

If you have used the tablespoon method to shape the rings, pat the dough into fairly smooth rings about 2 inches thick and an inch high, using a spatula. (Don't fuss over this—for me, one of the charms of these cheese rings is that no two ever look exactly alike.)

Glazing the Rings

In a small mixing bowl, beat the egg and 2 teaspoons of water with a whisk only long enough to combine them. Dip the pastry brush into the egg wash (as it is called) and lightly brush the entire surface of each ring. Don't allow any of the wash to drip down onto the baking sheets—

When the chou paste has been dropped from a spoon, use a spatula to pat surface moderately smooth.

this might prevent the rings from rising as high as they should. Sprinkle the remaining ¼ cup of freshly grated cheese evenly over the tops.

Baking and Serving the Rings

Set one cookie sheet on the upper shelf of the preheated 450° oven, the other sheet on the lower one. Bake the rings for 10 minutes, then lower the heat to 350° and bake for another 20 minutes. After a total of 40 minutes, the rings should be well puffed and light golden brown in color, and they should feel firm to the touch.

Slide them off their sheets onto a large platter and serve them at once. Or, if you prefer, cool the rings to lukewarm on a wire cake rack before serving them. To serve, either cut or tear the rings into pieces.

In French bakeries this spectacular cream-filled ring is called Paris-Brest and is, in fact, one of the great baking specialties of Paris. Although it is traditionally filled with sweetened vanilla-flavored whipped cream, or crème Chantilly as the French call it, you may wish to flavor the cream in other ways.

You might, for example, fold a teaspoonful or more of instant powdered coffee into the cream after it has been whipped. Or, if you are as addicted to almonds as I am, you might add a small handful of ground almonds to the cream, or even substitute a small amount of almond extract for the vanilla flavoring.

Almond-topped Whipped Cream Ring

Serves 6 to 8

THE RING:
1 recipe *Chou* Paste, page 89

FOR PREPARING THE PAN:
1 tablespoon butter
2 tablespoons unsifted flour

THE GLAZE AND TOPPING:
1 egg
2 teaspoons water
4 tablespoons blanched almonds,
    cut into slivers

THE FILLING:
2 cups chilled heavy cream
2 tablespoons sugar
2 teaspoons vanilla

FOR DUSTING:
1 tablespoon confectioners' sugar

Preheating the Oven

Slide one of your oven shelves into the middle slot of the oven; then set the thermostat at 450° and preheat the oven for 15 minutes.

Preparing the Pan

Using a pastry brush, the tablespoon of softened butter, and the 2 tablespoons of flour, grease and flour a cookie sheet. Then invert the sheet and rap it sharply on a table to knock off all of the excess flour, leaving only the thinnest of layers clinging to the buttered surface of the cookie sheet.

Using an inverted round 9-inch baking pan as a guide, press the outline of a circle firmly onto the floured surface of the cookie sheet.

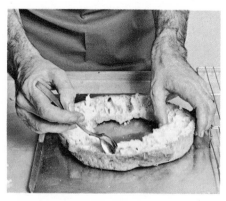

When almond-topped ring has cooled slightly, cut it in two horizontally with sawing motions of knife.

Using a spoon, scrape out the moist paste inside the two halves, then let the halves cool completely.

Making the Ring

Place heaping tablespoonfuls of the *chou* paste close together around the outside of the circle. Then, using a spatula, shape the dough into a fairly smooth ribbon about 2½ inches wide and 1½ inches high. (Don't fuss with this too much—one charm of this confection is its irregular surface.)

Alternatively, you may use a pastry bag and a plain No. 9 tip to pipe the *chou* paste into a similarly sized circle on the cookie sheet; in this case, no smoothing of the result will be needed.

Glazing the Ring

In a small mixing bowl, beat the egg and 2 teaspoons of water with a whisk only long enough to combine them well; do not overbeat the mixture.

Dip a pastry brush into the egg wash (as it is called) and lightly brush the entire surface of the ring, sides as well as top. Don't allow any of the wash to drip down onto the baking sheet—should this happen, it might prevent the ring from rising as high as it should. Sprinkle the ring with 4 tablespoons of slivered almonds, distributing them evenly over the entire surface of the ring, sides as well as top.

Baking the Ring

Set the cookie sheet in the preheated 450° oven and bake the ring undisturbed for 10 minutes, then lower the heat to 350° and bake it for another 10 minutes. At this

After sweetened whipped cream is piped into base, the top is replaced and sugar is dusted over it.

point, reduce the heat to 325° and bake the ring for 20 minutes more. After a total of 40 minutes it should be well puffed and a light golden brown in color, and it should feel firm to the touch.

Turn off the oven and remove the ring. Pierce its sides with the point of a small sharp knife at intervals of about 2 inches to release the enclosed steam.

Return the ring to the oven and let it dry for another 5 minutes with the oven door closed, then slide it off the cookie sheet and onto a cake rack and cool it for about 10 minutes.

With a large (preferably serrated) knife, slice the ring in two horizontally, using small sawing motions and making the cut closer to the top of the ring than to the bottom. With a tablespoon, scrape out any moist dough. Let the halves of the ring cool completely on a cake rack before filling them.

Making the Filling

In a chilled 2-quart bowl, beat 2 cups of chilled heavy cream with a rotary beater for a minute or two, or until it begins to thicken slightly. Add 2 tablespoons of sugar and 2 teaspoons of vanilla and continue beating until the cream forms firm but still slightly wavering peaks on the beater when it is lifted.

Gently set the base of the ring on a serving platter, and, using a spatula, pile the whipped cream into it. (Or use your pastry bag and the No. 9 star tip to pipe the cream into ornamental swirls.) The whipped cream should rise about 1 inch above the edge. Carefully set the top half over the filling like a crown. If you haven't used the pastry bag, swirl the cream on the sides into a pattern, using a spoon or a spatula.

Serving the Ring

Ideally, the ring should be served at once; refrigerate it if you must, but do not let it rest longer than half an hour or the cream will turn the pastry soggy.

Just before serving, dust the ring with the tablespoonful of confectioners' sugar, shaking it out of a perforated canister if you have one; or use a small sifter or fine sieve to distribute it evenly.

Acknowledgments

We wish to thank the following firms for providing accessories
   for use in the photographs:
B. Altman & Co., Fifth Ave. and 34th St., New York, N.Y. 10016
Ginori Fifth Avenue, 711 Fifth Ave., New York, N.Y. 10022
Hammacher-Schlemmer, 147 East 57th St., New York, N.Y. 10022
Flowers by James McNair of Terrestris Fifth Avenue,
   767 Fifth Ave., New York, N.Y. 10022

Cooking Adventures with Michael Field

Helen Witty, *Editor*

Bill Smith, Jr., *Art Director*

John David, *Photographer*

Jack Woolhiser, *Line Drawings*

Reisie Lonette, *Decorative Drawings*

Mary McCabe Gandall, *Editorial and Testing*
Assistant to Michael Field